A Book About Blockchain

A Book About Blockchain

How Companies Can Adopt Public Blockchain to Leap into the Future

Rajat Rajbhandari, PhD

BEP

BUSINESS EXPERT PRESS

Leader in applied, concise business books

A Book About Blockchain: How Companies Can Adopt Public Blockchain to Leap into the Future

First published in 2021 by
Business Expert Press, LLC
222 East 46th Street, New York, NY 10017
www.businessexpertpress.com

ISBN-13: 978-1-95334-938-5 (paperback)
ISBN-13: 978-1-63742-320-2 (hardcover)
ISBN-13: 978-1-95334-939-2 (e-book)

Business Expert Press Business Law and Corporate Risk Management Collection

Collection ISSN: 2333-6722 (print)
Collection ISSN: 2333-6730 (electronic)

Cover design by Dishebh Shrestha and interior design by S4Carlisle Publishing Services Private Ltd., Chennai, India

First edition: 2021

10 9 8 7 6 5 4 3 2 1

Advanced Quotes for *A Book About Blockchain*

I am impressed by the deep conceptual understanding that Rajat has. In this book, he conveys to the reader a practical, down-to-earth version of blockchain with all its elements.

As a business leader, and someone who pushed the envelope in applying technology to the resources industry, I view this book as perhaps the simplest end-to-end explanation of blockchain. It is a must read for any leader/ startup entrepreneur or consultant.

—Ricardo Escobar (Former CIO BHP Billiton)

It is quite simply the best book about blockchain for corporate executives. It will prove invaluable to early adopting project managers, strategists, and IT professionals as corporations experiment with blockchain and digital currencies. It perfectly nails the sweet spot between breathless hype over the technology's enormous potential and a too deep technical dive.

**—Chris Ballinger (CEO and Founder of MOBI),
Former Chief Financial Officer of Toyota Research Institute**

Rajat's technical understanding and real-world experience allows him to pierce the hype bubble to deliver a sober look at the promise of blockchain. This is an important book for professionals evaluating blockchain technology and its implications for their businesses.

—Patrick Duffy, President of Blockchain in Transport Alliance

Description

Executives, consultants, and strategists are wondering how to participate in the blockchain economy. They are wondering whether new business models that will emerge because of this novel technology will disrupt theirs or whether they will ignore their businesses and create completely different models. In this book I attempt to answer those questions. By the time you finish, you will understand what blockchain economy is, how to participate in it, and avoid being disrupted or, even worse, ignored. Drawing from my own experiences as research scientist and entrepreneur, the book describes methods to transform existing business by using digitized trust that is industrialized at scale.

Keywords

Blockchain; trust machine; smart contract; autonomous networks; consensus mechanisms; non fungible digital tokens; cryptocurrencies; tokenized platforms; decentralized autonomous organization; crypto governance; horizontal business innovation; risk management; interoperability.

Contents

Acknowledgments

A Book About Blockchain would not have been possible without the support of my family. They shared my belief that writing this book was a once-in-a-lifetime opportunity and a novel way to share my experience with others. They tolerated me locking myself in a room for hours during nights and weekends. The dexFreight family kept me motivated – Hector Hernandez, Ricardo Escobar, Adrian Giannini, Jim Handoush, Renat Khasanshyn. Also, special thanks to Ginger Goodin, Juan Carlo Villa, Art Richards, Hector Monsegur, Chris Ballinger, Santosh Shrestha, Rana Basu, Jorge Murillo, Dominik Batz, Ocean Protocol team, MOBI team, RSK and IOV Labs team. Much of this book is a result of experiences, heated discussions, and consultations we shared. I am grateful to Ken Melendez for proofreading the manuscript and Dishebh Shrestha for an amazing cover design and to the eSatya team for sponsoring the book website. Finally, I would not have started the book if my brother-in-law and a fellow blockchain enthusiast, Ruchin Singh, had not one day said to me, "Why don't you write a book about blockchain?"

A Personal Preface

Dear Readers,

Are you a c-level executive, consultant, architect, strategist, program manager wondering how you can participate in the blockchain economy? Are you thinking about transforming your businesses and implementing changes in your organization? Are you wondering if new business models that will emerge because of this novel technology will disrupt yours? Or will the technology ignore your business and create completely new ones? This book answers these questions and more at a fundamental level in a way an executive can understand. By the time you've finished the book, you'll understand what the blockchain economy is, how to participate in it, and avoid being disrupted or, worse, ignored. You need a playbook to not only transform but also architect your existing business into a new digital economy, the one in which trust is industrialized at scale.

This book is also about my personal journey and the challenges I faced as an entrepreneur in blockchain space. A significant portion of this book includes my own experiences as a researcher, CEO, CIO, and a startup cofounder. This book will help you "short circuit" the challenges I faced and remove obstacles for you early in the process of transforming your business.

I learned about blockchain in early 2013 but never bothered to inquire about it. When the first Decentralized Autonomous Organization (DAO) was hacked, in June 2016, I started to look seriously into why it was hacked. Note: to learn more about the hack, please read "The DAO, the hack, the soft fork, and the hard fork" published in cryptocompare.com.[1] I'm not a security expert by any stretch of the imagination, but the idea of somebody hacking an autonomous organization was intriguing.

---

[1] CryptoCompare. June 2, 2018. "The Dao, the Hack, the Soft Fork and the Hard Fork," *CryptoCompare*. https://www.cryptocompare.com/coins/guides/the-dao-the-hack-the-soft-fork-and-the-hard-fork/.

What is an autonomous organization? What was the flaw in the DAO's smart contract? How did the smart contract function? To understand how it was hacked, I had to learn about smart contracts at the fundamental level. This took me to Vitalik Buterin's white paper on Ethereum first published in 2013.[2]

Unlike most people, who learned about blockchain via Bitcoin, I learned about it because of smart contracts. Back then, I was not a huge believer in Bitcoin compared with now. I did not see Bitcoin making a significant contribution to business process improvement.

I wanted to know how blockchain worked at the code level and was drawn to Andreas Antonopoulos' book *Mastering Bitcoin* published in December 2014.[3] The book helped me understand nuances and intricacies of how Bitcoin worked and the fundamentals of blockchain itself. Light bulbs went off in my head everywhere after I read the book. Shortly thereafter, I read Satoshi Nakamoto's white paper several times.[4] The engineer in me said that I had to understand the fundamentals and go straight to the source.

I learned more, wrote code, and had long discussions with friends about the technology. In 2017 I published a report describing how blockchain will revolutionize the transportation and mobility industries. At this point I was on a roll. I was invited to dozens of events and delivered talks to several companies. I also moderated and spoke on multiple blockchain panels. I felt a sense of obligation to speak on stage at those events. Each event motivated me (and still does), giving me a sense of purpose to educate others about blockchain's fundamentals and theory. I developed a passion to evangelize blockchain to groups of people

[2]V. Buterin. 2013. "A Next Generation Smart Contract and Decentralized Application Platform," *Ethereum Foundation*.

[3]A. Antonopoulos. 2014. *Mastering Bitcoin: Unlocking Digital Currencies* (New York, NY: O'Reilly Media.)

[4]S. Nakamoto. 2008. "Bitcoin: A Peer-to-Peer Electronic Cash System," *Bitcoin.org*.

at conferences and summits. In return, I learned about their pain points, blind spots in workflow, internal issues being discussed at the c-level, their concerns about challenging environments to implement blockchain, and much more.

That was not enough. I wanted to do something bigger.

In early 2018 I decided to jump ship and left the comfort of academia and cofounded dexFreight to utilize blockchain in the logistics industry. I did it partly because of what some experts call "crypto-secession." It means leaving/rejecting the current corporate structure of centralized power to a decentralized organization. I say "partly" because I still believe in existing corporate structure; however, I wanted to explore what potentials of this new and alternate power structure built on blockchain.

While I was having this discussion with my brother-in-law, he said, why don't you write a book about your experience as an entrepreneur in blockchain. So, I did, and much of this book is a catalog of those experiences. Every piece of this book contains thoughts that passed through my brain at some point, while some are experiences I encountered along the way while cofounding dexFreight. Hence, everything in this book reflects my own opinions and no one else's.

Along this journey, I met individuals moving into blockchain—some left their cushy jobs or were on the verge of leaving. Some are still working their old jobs but wish to introduce blockchain into their company. I have seen their struggle because I've experienced them myself. I dedicate this book to my new friends who jumped into the rabbit hole. The brave men and women who right now are on the brink of leaving a cushy six-figure job and, like myself, say goodbye to colleagues and pursue a journey toward the unchartered territory of blockchain. Each one of them will dive into the rabbit hole to start a blockchain startup, become a blockchain consultant, or pivot a company to begin using blockchain technology.

I will call them brave because it takes a certain amount of resolve to take that giant leap of faith. I know how it feels, because I did it. I took that giant leap of faith, started a blockchain startup, and became a blockchain evangelist. I also refuse to judge people on the basis of how they want to use blockchain—integrate it with their existing system and turn it into something more powerful or create a decentralized system that goes against the ethos of power centralization. To me, blockchain is a free-at-will technology. This book is not about learning the fundamentals of blockchain, because there are plenty of books, blogs, and videos out there for that. In fact, I assume you already know a thing or two about blockchain and how it works.

I didn't want to write a book on how blockchain will change the world and everything around us. Let's leave that to notable writers and thinkers like Don Tapscott, Melanie Swan, William Mougayar, and many more. I also didn't want to write about algorithms and mathematics of blockchain. Instead, I felt executives, managers, strategists, designers, and consultants who operate between the 100,000-ft level of thinkers and the 100-ft level of developers need a different kind of reference, one that will assist them in developing and implementing actual business models using the most pragmatic approach.

I wanted to write a book that takes a more pragmatic approach to blockchain's possibilities in transforming existing business models and creating new ones. For example, if you have read news headlines in 2017 or 2018, you would have thought smart contracts have solved all the problems in the legal domain. Well, guess what? They haven't even scratched the surface yet. At the same time, smart contracts are creating new possibilities that were not feasible before.

In addition to understanding the fundamentals, executives need to know how to transform their businesses while implementing changes in their organization to make it happen. They will face strict challenges such as the harsh reality of implementing blockchain—the same way I did. They need a book to understand the power of the public blockchain economy, and, most importantly, how to participate in it and avoid being outdated. They need a book to gradually transition from *why* to *how*—a guide that explains how to leap into the future enabled by blockchain. So, here it is.

Sincerely,

Rajat

Dallas, Texas

CHAPTER 1

Introduction

Foundational technologies like blockchain take decades to make a massive impact on society and economy. However, if you had read the news, you would not have believed it. The hype machine was real, and the message was that the technology would not go through a natural cycle of development. Instead, it will rapidly disrupt everything. This continuous news cycle declared that blockchain will solve problems in finance, supply chain, election, insurance, and more. The blockchain will soon drive the global economy, and the disruption was well underway.

In 2017 and 2018, blockchain startups raised billions from crypto millionaires, venture capitalists, and other institutional investors via initial coin offerings. The market valued 1-year-old blockchain protocols of several billion dollars, without a single practical use case. Executives were ready to pay thousands of dollars to attend conferences to understand what this new technology was about. Conferences charged accordingly to listen to "so-called" investors because they had a few million dollars in their crypto wallets. These conferences featured blockchain experts, who cannot explain with a straight face what a smart contract was. However, hype is not all that bad because reality always sets in thereafter. In 2019, when projects failed, the market pushed scammers out in the open. Investors who poured billions on protocols began pushing for implementation of real-world use cases. The new paradigm steered the blockchain technology to a proper course of true innovation and scaling.

In 2020 people started talking about scaling blockchain applications. Use cases that could scale widely became important for startups and investors. The paradigm of blockchain as being a trustless machine changed to a trust machine. It is a trust at industrial scale. The true potential of blockchain is to reduce information asymmetry between parties using immutable ledgers anchored on an open network that operates globally using an open protocol.

Blockchain is a revolutionary technology, and, like other revolutionary technologies, it will not disrupt existing business models but ignore them and create innovative ones we have not seen before. I describe these innovative business models later in the book. These innovative business models will challenge the existing ones and even become a viable alternative, the same way cryptocurrency is challenging traditional finance.

In due course, existing businesses, especially the smart ones, will grow and start adopting blockchain (along with other nascent technologies) because they will want to stay relevant and transform. This book provides you with three key ingredients to implement blockchain and take part in the new economy by helping understand the fundamental components of blockchain, risks, and challenges of innovative business models, and ways to take part in the blockchain world. After reading the book, you'll be able to evangelize the use of blockchain within your organization and with your customers, design breakthrough and innovative business models, and analyze risks and opportunities—legal, administrative, and technical.

CHAPTER 2

Evangelizing Blockchain

In November 2017 I stood in front of over 500 executives from logistics and supply chain companies who had gathered to hear about blockchain during the inaugural event of Blockchain in Transportation Alliance. This was my first stint as a blockchain evangelical. I didn't know a lot about it as I do now. But it was enough to put me on stage. After 20 minutes of blockchain 101, a flurry of questions came at me. What do you mean by public as in public blockchain? What is a consensus? When should I buy Bitcoin? It's not going to work in logistics until we standardize data, correct?

I could tell there was a lot of curiosity in the room, although 90 percent of attendees didn't fully understand the meaning of consensus, mining, hash, and so forth. Otherwise, they wouldn't have made the trip. They were there to find out what this new thing is that everyone is talking about. I also made a point toward the end by saying there are massive potentials for disruption in the industry. All it will require is that you understand the fundamentals of blockchain and evangelize within your company, community, and peer group.

How Should One Evangelize Blockchain?

What I mean by evangelizing is being ready to go to a conference room full of strangers, bosses, colleagues, or customers and convince them why implementing blockchain is a smart idea. First off, you need to believe in the technology. Guy Kawasaki, in a recent blog post, stated, "If you don't love it, don't evangelize it."[1] Blockchain evangelists must do three things now when the technology is in its infancy—educate, inspire, and defend.

---

[1]G. Kawasaki. April 29, 2014. "Art of Evangelism," *Guykawasaki.com*. https://guykawasaki.com/the-art-of-evangelism/.

Educate—Even though the technology has been around for almost 10 years and parts of it even older (e.g., cryptography, distributed systems), many in noncrypto industries are just now beginning to understand what it means and how it operates. When I organize blockchain 101, I still get asked questions such as "what is mining and is there somebody (a human) sitting in front of a computer validating all of the transactions?" And I end up spending a good chunk of time answering trivial questions.

I always make a point that however trivial those questions might be, they ought to be answered because understanding the fundamentals is critical to the technology's adoption. If people have too many lingering questions and are stuck in fundamentals, they will feel like they've reached a dead end, which may kill their enthusiasm to move forward.

That's one of the reasons I have not done and refuse to do YouTube videos or video tutorials. Instead, I prefer classroom and conference settings where participants are open and ask trivial questions.

Another reason education is important for adoption is that people can then cut through the hype and clearly separate strengths and weaknesses of blockchain. It is obvious that when people have a better understanding of something, they can make more informed decisions around it. Decisions about implementing blockchain inside a boardroom are not going to happen by simply saying, "Everybody is doing it; we should do it too."

Inspire—Empowering an individual or an organization is another critical factor in blockchain's adoption. However, empowerment comes only after education and awareness of the technology's strengths and weaknesses as well as its core capabilities or usefulness. Each individual or organization should be able to see clearly whether they possess an opportunity or a threat.

Defend—When a technology is in its early stages, it comes under attack from all sides. Are you prepared to defend its position? Do you have enough willpower and firepower to do so, considering that it needs defenders and caretakers? Electricity, cars, telecommunication, and the Internet all came under tremendous attack from the status quo when those technologies were in their early stages. Add in a bit of history and incidents to colorize the point.

People who like the status quo will attack it by associating Bitcoin with pornography, terrorists, hackers, and drug dealers. If you perform a Google search, there are many articles in the mainstream media about blockchain being nothing but a fad that allows child pornographers to store porn along with Bitcoin. They will argue that it allows terrorists to buy weapons and hackers to blackmail their victims. The media will say, "Haven't you heard of Silk Road?"

How do you defend against those blatant attacks? It's easy. Give them the truth that they can't swallow. Kenneth Rogoff, a Harvard professor, argued in his book, *The Curse of Cash*, that 80 percent of domestically held cash is used for criminal activities and tax evasion.[2] A whopping 93 percent of the U.S. dollar notes are tainted with cocaine.[3] Each bill didn't necessarily change hands with drug dealers and users, because some of them got tainted via teller machines.

Ask the media to find a corner drug dealer that accepts Bitcoin. Ask them for evidence that a known terrorist group bought weapons using cryptocurrency or uses blockchain to organize their operation. They don't exist yet. Even if they do exist, so what? Technology, governments, traditional institutions all take part (knowingly and unknowingly) in criminal activities. Criminals are always the first to exploit the technology and the government.

The reasons are obvious. They operate in a highly competitive and risky environment. They will always be on the lookout for bleeding edge technology to beat their competition and law enforcement. Believe it or not, porn made the Internet what it is today. They were the early adopters of image and video compression technologies and created the best-performing websites before big corporations did.

In "The Truth about Blockchain," published in *Harvard Business Review*, authors Lansiti and Lakhani declared blockchain as a foundational technology,[4] and described it as having the potential to create new foundations for our economic and social systems. Instead of disrupting

---

[2]K. Rogoff. 2017. *The Curse of Cash: How Large-Denomination Bills Aid Crime and Tax Evasion and Constrain Monetary Policy* (Princeton, NJ: Princeton University Press).

[3]A. Negrusz, J. Perry, and C. Moore. 1998. "Detection of Cocaine on Various Denominations of United States Currency," *Journal of Forensic Science* 43, no. 3, pp. 626-29.

[4]M. Lansiti and K. Lakhani. 2018. "The Truth about Blockchain," *Harvard Business Review*. https://hbr.org/2017/01/the-truth-about-blockchain.

traditional business models, foundational technologies create innovative business opportunities that did not exist before. Transmission control protocol/Internet protocol (TCP/IP) sparked the creation of the World Wide Web, leading to the commercial Internet boom introducing e-commerce, music, and video streaming that utilizes large networks of users spanning regions and continents. Applications based on a foundational technology often take a long time to emerge and become mainstream.

The adoption process of foundational technologies such as blockchain is gradual, incremental, and steady, unlike the classic hockey stick adoption we typically associate with disruptive innovations.[5] Foundational innovations must overcome technological, organizational, governance, and political barriers. Although the impact of blockchain could be enormous, its transformational impact is decades away.

Your blockchain company's success, or your success as a consultant, depends not only on how amazing your offering is, but also on how quickly your customers understand and accept this new technology. How do you approach them to say that the technology works and will work to solve their problem? Good evangelists not only believe in the technology and defend it, but also have experience doing it. To be credible, you first need to have spent significant time with people, wrestling with their real-world problems.[6]

One Person's Hype Is Another Person's Headache

Hypes about technologies can be powerful and can trigger an innovation race attracting funding and favorable regulations.[7] Technological hypes are an extreme manifestation of expectations. We often refer to Gartner's

---

[5]I. Wladawsky-Berger. January 20, 2017. "The Internet, Blockchain, and the Evolution of Foundational Innovations," *The Wall Street Journal.* https://blogs.wsj.com/cio/2017/01/20/the-internet-blockchain-and-the-evolution-of-foundational-innovations/.

[6]T. Elliott. July 20, 2013. "How to Become a Technology Evangelist," *Digital Business and Business Analytics.* https://timoelliott.com/blog/2013/07/how-to-become-a-technology-evangelist.html.

[7]S. Bakker and B. Budde. 2012. "Technological Hype and Disappointment: Lessons from the Hydrogen and Fuel Cell Case," *Technology Analysis & Strategic Management* 24, no. 6, pp. 549-63.

hype cycle to know which technology is going through which phase of the hype cycle.

If you are curious, blockchain is falling into the "trough of disillusionment" as of 2017, according to Gartner.[8] Blockchain first appeared in the Gartner hype cycle in 2016 in his piece "Peak of Inflated Expectation." Even Gartner didn't see it coming in years prior to that.

Fueling the blockchain hype, there are at least a dozen books for sale on Amazon, as well as hundreds of news articles and blogs, about how blockchain will disrupt every business and change the world on a large scale. I've read a lot of these publications, and they helped me become a blockchain believer. Yet, because of my strong academic background, I found myself looking for evidence. No one, just yet, has put the pieces of that evidence together. In that regard, I'm a skeptic and like to question the hype at every opportunity I get. I do strongly believe that blockchain will cause significant disruption and change many businesses for the better.

Businesses that have existed for decades will take decades to come to an end. When their livelihoods are at stake, they tend to fight back. If they can't win, they will evolve. Obviously, not all businesses will succeed. Uber was supposed to take over the taxi industry and has not done so. Airbnb was supposed to disrupt the hotel industry. Hotels are, in fact, doing better, as reflected by their stock performance. Amazon was supposed to kill malls and brick and mortar stores. Yes, some have died, but smart ones have consolidated, fought back, and are still doing OK.

Will Bitcoin and other cryptocurrencies kill banks anytime soon? No, but that is irrelevant. Cryptocurrencies will create a new customer base that didn't need or have access to banks in the first place. Will blockchain remove notary publics? Yes, many of them. It doesn't matter because most notary publics draw their income from alternate sources. It doesn't matter to them that their stamps are suddenly useless. Will blockchain remove logistics brokers? Yes and no. A few smart brokers will adopt blockchain and provide customers better service at a lower price point.

---

[8]Garter. July, 2017. "Gartner Hype Cycle for Emerging Technologies 2017," *Gartner*. https://blogs.gartner.com/smarterwithgartner/files/2017/08/Emerging-Technology-Hype-Cycle-for-2017_Infographic_R6A.jpg.

It is convenient to believe that blockchain will increase business efficiency and disrupt many things for the better. However, I refuse to blindly accept the concept without evidence that must arrive in the coming years. For now, my everyday effort is to stay away from the hype and be upfront with the community that widespread adoption of blockchain is a long-term play.

Gartner surveyed 3,000 chief information officers and asked them, "What are your organization's plans in terms of blockchain?" Only 1 percent said they had any kind of blockchain adoption within their organizations.[9] To go from 1 percent to 99 percent adoption is a long-term game that will take a few generations. I don't believe the technology will leapfrog in the next few years until we've all experienced and overcome the hurdles and then passed those experiences to the next generation.

There is no question that blockchain is currently in a bubble. Steve Wozniak, the cofounder of Apple, warned that "[e]arly adopters can burn themselves out by not being prepared to be stable in the long run."[10] If I'm correct in interpreting his comment, early adopters like us should be ready to face destabilizing market forces before blockchain is widely adopted. Market forces, in my opinion, will be pushed back by the status quo, culture, and a better user experience. I do not buy the argument that the technology is too immature for adoption; it is simply not 100 percent user friendly.

Anoop Nannra, head of CISCO's blockchain initiative, made an interesting comment on CNBC, in May 2018, to the effect that widespread adoption of blockchain is anyone's guess because it involves shifting business' mindset and that to accomplish it will take generations.[11] If we combine statements by Mr. Wozniak and Mr. Nannra together, getting over the status quo will require future generations to implement blockchain.

---

[9]A. Loten. May 4, 2018. "Amid Blockchain Hype, Few Deployments, Limited Interest, Survey Finds." *The Wall Street Journal.* https://blogs.wsj.com/cio/2018/05/04/amid-blockchain-hype-few-deployments-limited-interest-survey-finds/.

[10]"Blockchain Hype Overstates Reality, Says Steve Wozniak," *Bitcoin Magazine.* https://bitcoinmagazine.com/articles/blockchain-hype-overstates-reality-says-steve-wozniak/, (accessed August 4, 2018).

[11]E. Cheng. June 4, 2018. "For all the Hype, Blockchain Applications are Still Years, Even Decades Away," *CNBC.* https://www.cnbc.com/2018/06/04/for-all-the-hype-blockchain-applications-are-still-years-even-decades-away.html.

Maximalist from the Inside, "Whatever Works" from the Outside

I used to be an open blockchain maximalist. I argued with myself and others that private blockchain did not have any future. I still believe that is the case, but it will be at least a decade before we see a complete demise of private blockchain, the same way the intranet took years to vanish.

As I interacted more with companies and enterprises, I came to realize that there is nothing crazy about letting companies use enterprise blockchain to collaborate with other companies to solve common business problems. The main argument is one of control, because no one enjoys giving up their power. After decades of using centralized databases with fully controlled access and visibility, there is no way companies would suddenly shred their hesitation to send transactions through an open blockchain.

The more I helped companies ideate blockchain implementation, the more I saw them get cozy with the idea of hybrid designs. Hybrid designs are when some aspects of the transactions such as identity or account information are stored in centralized databases. Transaction finality such as asset transfer or milestones in critical workflow are added to open blockchains such as Ethereum and Bitcoin.

Another reason I stopped arguing against enterprise blockchain is all the marketing hype created by companies such as IBM, SAP, and Accenture. Promoting their blockchain platforms has helped startups like ours spend less time educating executives about the value propositions of blockchain. When we showcased dexFreight at an ICO Summit in California, we were well received by the crowd that stopped by our booth.

The companies we worked with had no clue how logistics and supply chain worked, but they had read the constant stream of news from IBM, Walmart, and Maersk pilot projects regarding the utilization of blockchain to create a highly visible supply chain. It was free publicity for little guys like us. IBM executives were pleasantly surprised when I told them to keep up the hype machine while attending a blockchain event in Dallas in 2018. Hype isn't necessarily bad, but companies must make an additional effort to separate the hype from nonsense.

Defending Cryptocurrencies

Early on, I was cautioned by my colleagues not to talk about cryptocurrencies at a blockchain panel during a logistics conference. They said that Bitcoin has a bad reputation and that there is no need to talk about the digital asset itself. Cryptocurrencies are bad; they have no purpose. Let's only talk about blockchain, they suggested.

Over time, I made a point during these panels that talking about the history of blockchain is important and that Bitcoin was the first use case of blockchain technology. Not only that, but Bitcoin should not be viewed merely as an esoteric cryptocurrency. Bitcoin is a reference implementation that sets the foundation for people to build other platforms and applications, including the smart contracts blockchain, Ethereum. Without Bitcoin, Ethereum and its smart contract abilities may not exist today.

I come out in full force to talk about why cryptocurrencies exist, not simply from an economic standpoint, but also touching upon securitization, rewards, and payment proxies to sustain the public blockchain. Without an underlying cryptocurrency, there is no economic incentive to keep the public blockchain secured.

Real Potential of Blockchain: Reduce Information Asymmetry?

This book has numerous examples of blockchain's value propositions and business potentials. These value propositions are being proven every day and will continue. However, I kept struggling to answer why and what is blockchain's potential at its core. Until I stumbled upon an article written by Lauri Auronen on the theory of asymmetric information.[12] This concept was introduced in the 1970s, and George Akerlof, Michael Spence, and Joseph Stiglitz received the Nobel Prize in Economic Sciences for the topic. The premise is simple. Between the two parties involved in a transaction, one always has more information than the other, or one party has better information than the other.

---

[12]L. Auronen. May 21, 2003. "Asymmetric Information: Theory and Applications," *Seminar in Strategy and International Business.* https://pdfs.semanticscholar.org/cdc1/10d48cfa54659f3a09620d51240f09cf1acc.pdf.

That is why we use real-estate brokers to reduce the information asymmetry while buying a house. The seller knows almost everything about the house. The seller has incentives to hide certain facts about the property and sell it quickly. The buyer, on the other hand, doesn't know much beyond visible attributes. Real-estate agents acting on behalf of the buyer will extract as much information about the property, including disputes, comparable market price, past liens, and so forth to reduce the information asymmetry in favor of the buyer.

Brokerages and marketplaces exist to reduce the asymmetry, for which they charge fees either from one or both parties. The same concept applies to money transfer between the two parties. Bitcoin showed that blockchain can, in fact, be used to reduce the intermediary fee by showing that both transacting parties have equal levels of information or full transparency that the transaction has been added to a ledger and both parties can see changes in balances. Both parties have equal access to the underlying ledger. It is not the case that the receiver has better access to the ledger than the sender or vice versa.

Smart contracts took that potential to the next level. They allowed parties to exchange tokens of different value without an intermediary because it was not required since both parties have near perfect symmetric information about the rate of exchange. This book largely follows the idea that smart contracts (and blockchain) will have a profound impact on commerce, considering their potential to reduce the asymmetry because both parties in a transaction can see the parameters coded in the contract and that the contract will execute without bias to either party.

CHAPTER 3

Explaining Blockchain Fundamentals

Key components that form blockchain technology have existed since long before Satoshi Nakamoto's white paper. As Mr. Antonopoulos put it in the book *Mastering Bitcoin,* "Bitcoin represents the culmination of decades of research in cryptography and distributed systems…". Prior works by Wei Dai, Hal Finney, Adam Back, and others while creating digital cash demonstrated how proof of work contributed to the creation of Bitcoin's components. Satoshi's contribution was to integrate these components to create Bitcoin, solving the age-old problem of consensus and double spending in distributed systems.

My goal for this chapter is to engage readers like yourself in a high-level discussion of what these components are, how they function, and what their purpose is within the blockchain ecosystem. My goal is not to delve too deeply into technical detail. In the next few sections, I present theories and concepts behind blockchain in a way understood by laymen and people who do not have the resources or the luxury of digesting underlying mathematics, algorithms, and the extended history preceding Bitcoin.

Blockchain technology has four key components: ledger of transactions, network of nodes, consensus mechanism, and cryptography.

Ledger of Transactions

A transaction means transferring assets from A to B, or Alice to Bob, and entering that simple piece of information into a distributed ledger. When asset transfer from Alice to Bob takes place, both parties must digitally sign the transaction. When both parties digitally sign, proof of original ownership and new ownership is declared. Individual transactions are time-stamped, creating a unique identification known as a digital hash.

Commerce and trade are about transferring assets from A to B while maintaining an immutable, or unchangeable, ledger to avoid double spending. Those assets may come in the form of money, goods, or services. Our society is constantly engaged in transferring assets (Bitcoin, cars, homes, money, data) from one entity to another.

To make those transactions official, we register them with a third party such as the government, banks, appraisal districts, lawyers, or notaries that both sender and receiver trust. The transaction is completed under the assumption that this "trusted" third party will not tamper with the transaction while keeping it safe, attesting to its validity when needed.

Transactions can be viewed as a set of data or decisions being passed along to complete a single workflow. Multiple agencies act as gatekeepers on the workflow, and they open and close gates based on pieces of information they receive. A simple example is boarding a flight. From a traveler's perspective, it is a single linear workflow from purchasing the ticket to boarding the flight. A travel agency provides the ticket after payment is received from that customer's credit card. At the gate once the airline representative checks the boarding pass and Transportation Security Administration performs their security check, you can then board the flight. The airline opens and closes the gates based on pieces of data provided by a trusted party.

Any digital transaction can be added to the blockchain, as shown in Figure 3.1. Transactions do not have to include the full attributes of data being passed along the workflow. Sometimes it can be simple verifications such as yes/no, or valid/invalid, as described in the preceding example.

Token transfer between parties
Approval of documents
Digital fingerprint of documents
Digital fingerprint of transactions
.... and more

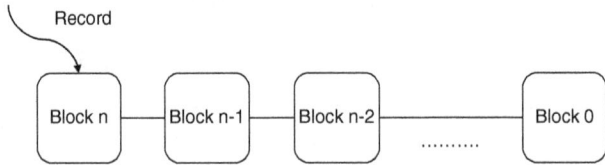

Record

Block n — Block n-1 — Block n-2 .... Block 0

Figure 3.1 Variety of digital transactions that can be added to the blocks in blockchain

What does a typical transaction look like in a public blockchain? I'm often asked by nontech people, "What does a transaction look like in blockchain?" It would be easy to say, "The same way it looks in a database with fields containing rows and columns," but that is not the case. Keep in mind that blockchain stores transactions from A to B and attributes of those transactions in chronologically ordered data blocks, as shown in Figure 3.2.

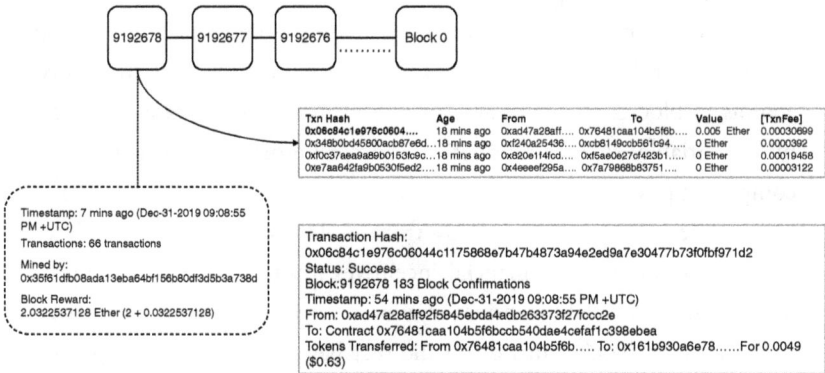

Figure 3.2 Transactions are hashed and added into a block using mining process

Whether to include or exclude the attribute of data along with decisions/verifications is a matter of application design. It's not recommended to include many different attributes in the blockchain if it is a public one, the reason being that public blockchain is not designed to hold large blocks of data attributes. The key value proposition of blockchain is to record whether a transaction has occurred or not within the respective network of nodes.

Network of Nodes

I believe that the key ingenuity of blockchain, as mentioned in Nakamoto's white paper, is the use of the peer-to-peer network of nodes. The network receives and then adds transactions into a chain of data blocks known as a distributed ledger. Instead of using trusted third-party entities, blockchain utilizes a network of nodes to register transactions, preventing double-spend transactions.

By broadcasting transactions to a network of independent nodes, they become computationally difficult to tamper without fallout or severe penalty from fellow participants in the network.

In open blockchain the number of nodes can be in the thousands because anybody can join and leave the network. Every participating node within the network constructs and maintains its own independent version of the blockchain based on a common set of rules; there is no need for nodes to know or trust each other. In private blockchain, the number of nodes is small because only preapproved participants can join the network.

The network, to operate as a tamperproof keeper of history, requires protocols that nodes and stakeholders abide by. Protocols are nothing but a set of rules governing how to broadcast, validate, and add transactions to blocks. Protocols are added and modified by many predetermined variables such as number of nodes, number of participants, and computing power.

In order to prevent somebody from unilaterally modifying transactions or forking blocks, financial incentives must be built into the protocol. Those financial incentives may be a direct monetary benefit used in many open blockchains or an indirect benefit used in many private blockchains. Indirect benefit can be in the form of privileges that come with being a participant of a network.

In open blockchains, incentive mechanisms are hardcoded into the network protocol. There are two major incentive mechanisms that provide for the security and immutability of the blockchain: block rewards and transaction fees. Such incentives also play a critical role in providing resilience to the blockchain. Special types of nodes, called mining nodes, are awarded with tokens, or underlying cryptocurrency, for expending computation power to achieve consensus.[1] Connections between different types of nodes are shown in Figure 3.3.

Block rewards get distributed to miners for successfully adding a new block of transactions to the network. A transaction fee is the sum of values of all inputs of the transaction minus the sum of values of all outputs created by the transaction. Private or permissioned blockchains do not necessarily need financial incentives baked in because network participants have enough incentives already just being active in the network. Also, network participants might be vetted and known to the rest of the participants.

---

[1]"Incentive Mechanisms for Securing the Bitcoin Blockchain," *BitFury Group*, December 07, 2015.

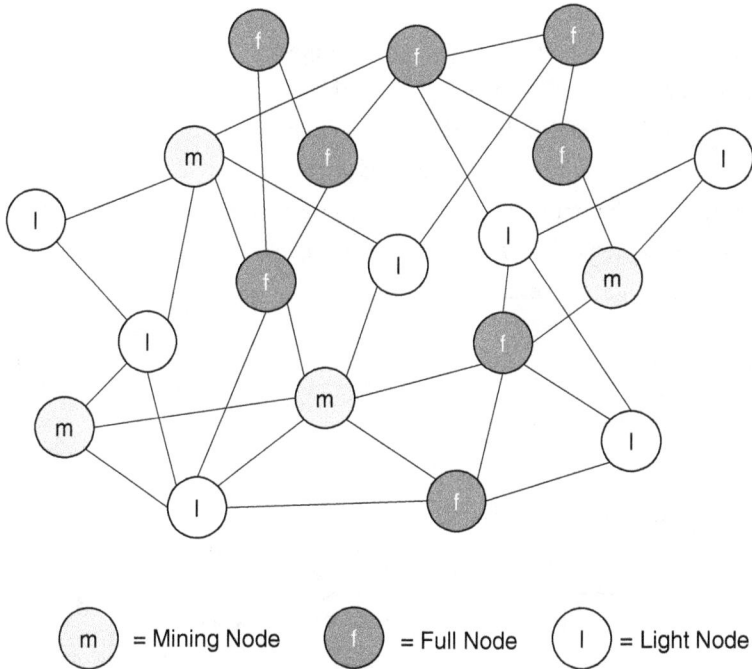

Figure 3.3 Mining, full, and light nodes are arbitrarily connected to each other

Cryptography

Blockchain technology relies on two key requirements to function properly without a centralized trusted entity. First, it needs to ensure that a transaction did originate from the sender with unique identification that can be verified. Second, it needs to ensure that past transactions cannot be tampered with and that the information stays authentic.

Centralized institutions perform these tasks by complying with legal and regulatory authority given to them and by using a strict hierarchy of checks and balances within the organization. In blockchain, instead of utilizing centralized institutions, cryptography and mathematics are used to perform those functions to "replace middlemen with mathematics."

Cryptography is a topic best explained by mathematicians and cryptographers. For ordinary folks, cryptography is the science of encrypting and decrypting information using mathematics to prevent unintended users from viewing private information.

The process of creating public and private keys as well as ensuring that transactions are verified by nodes is shown in Figure 3.4. First, every transaction needs to be digitally signed by valid keys, also known as the sender's private and public keys. The public key of the sender also becomes a digital address and is created from a private or secret key. The sender signs the transaction with a digital signature that is generated from the sender's private key. The digital signature relies on the assumption that the sender and receiver alike will keep the private key secret.

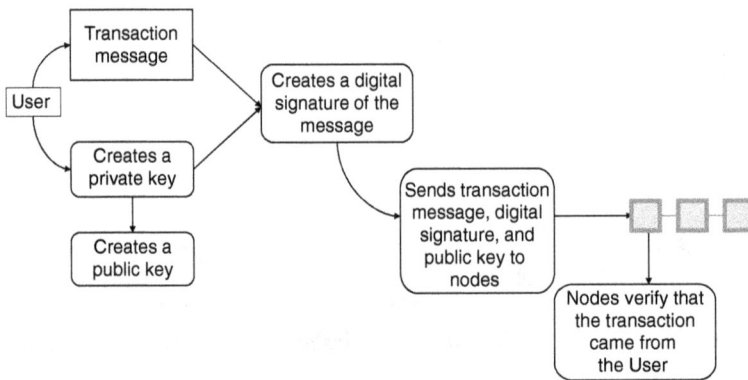

Figure 3.4 Users sign transactions with private key and verified by miners using public key

Because there is a mathematical relationship between public and private keys, the signature can be validated by the receiver against the sender's public key without revealing the sender's private key. The rest of the network also verifies that the transaction did in fact originate from the sender by his or her public key and signature.[2] Keys explain the first requirement for cryptography mentioned at the beginning of this section.

Consensus and Mining

Key to the operation of a blockchain is ensuring that the entire network, without centralized trust, agrees with the contents of the transactional

---

[2]A. Antonopoulos. 2015. *Mastering Bitcoin – Unlocking Digital Cryptocurrencies* (New York, NY: O'Reilly Media).

ledger. The participants in the network, without being told by a central authority to trust the ledger, conclude that the ledger, or history of transactions, has not been tampered with and that it is a valid copy of the ledger.

Traditionally, humans verify a ledger by manually validating transactions, reconciling with their own records, and raising their hands in a round table meeting to proclaim, "Yes, I attest that the ledger is valid." How do computers accomplish it? Reaching a consensus must be dynamic and automated so that transactions are continuously added to blocks without human intervention.

No matter what the consensus mechanism, it needs to accomplish three key tasks, also shown in Figure 3.5:

- Based on a predefined set of rules or protocol, verify each transaction broadcasted by a node to the network.
- Aggregate transactions into a block, verify new blocks proposed by nodes, and add blocks to a chain.
- Finally, select the longest chain to be the valid one, and prevent it from unnecessary forking.

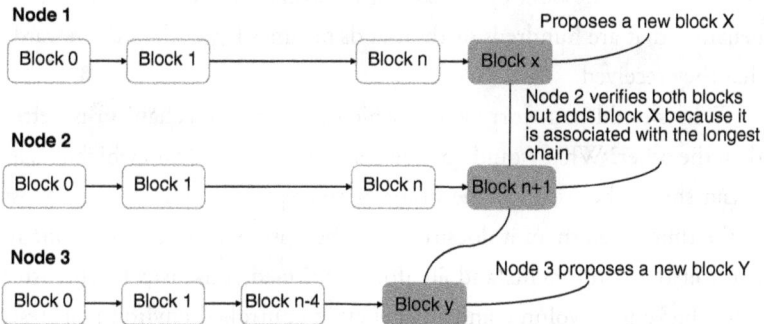

Figure 3.5 Nodes compete to include transactions and blocks

Because there is no central authority that directs all other nodes to arrive at a consensus, they must do so independently. How do the nodes manage to come into consensus without a central authority? In the case of Bitcoin and Ethereum, mining nodes play a cryptographic hash probability game, called Proof of Work, to win rewards and add their proposed block to the blockchain.

To win the game, a mining node must guess a number, called a *nonce*, that, in combination with all the previous data in the blockchain, outputs a hash (or digital fingerprint) when run through the Secure Hash Algorithm (SHA-256) function.[3] A cryptographic hash function takes data and translates it into a very long string of letters and numbers. The first mining node to guess the correct nonce wins the right to create the next block. Only a certain nonce combined with the correct previously verified blockchain data will result in the correct hash. If inaccurate or fraudulent previous records are input, the correct hash cannot be guessed.

Proof of Work is the most well-known consensus mechanism used by Bitcoin, Ethereum, and Dash, to name a few. Among other consensus mechanisms are Proof of Stake, Delegated Proof of Stake, and Proof of Elapsed Time.[4] The Proof of Work mechanism has gone through more market, technical, and intellectual scrutiny than other mechanisms. Ethereum, starting Version 2.0, is moving into Proof of Stake consensus.

Proof of Stake does not rely on rewards for security but rather on penalties. Validators put money ("deposits") at stake and are rewarded as compensation for locking up their capital and maintaining nodes. Validators are also rewarded for taking extra precautions to ensure their private key safety, but the bulk of the cost of reverting transactions comes from penalties that are hundreds or thousands of times larger than the rewards that they received.

Why should you worry about which consensus mechanism is better than the other? What would you say if a customer asked you which mechanism should be used for the proof of concept or a pilot project? Most of the time, I tell them it doesn't matter because test projects are done in controlled environments and all aforementioned consensus mechanisms can achieve high volume and frequency in controlled environment tests with a limited number of test nodes.

---

[3] I. Simpson. September 19, 2017. "To Understand Blockchain, You Should Understand Cryptographic Hashes First," *Medium Corporation*. https://medium.com/vandal-press/to-understand-blockchains-you-should-understand-cryptographic-hashes-first-for-normies-93bc7645e816

[4] A. Rosic. "Basic Primer: Blockchain Consensus Protocol," *Blockgeeks*. https://blockgeeks.com/guides/blockchain-consensus/, (accessed August 05, 2018).

We will see additional consensus mechanisms enter the ecosystem, including the improvements to existing ones such as Lightning and Plasma. We no longer exist in the heyday of consensus mechanisms owing to increased development and adoption worldwide.

I am often asked, "Who pays for mining if I deploy smart contracts and send transactions?" "Do I have to pay the mining fees?" Although this sounds like a novice question, it is, in fact, legitimate for those who operate end-user centric platforms. The end users are not well-versed with public blockchains such as Ethereum and Bitcoin and how participants are financially incentivized. Hence, if you are familiar with it, feel free to skip this section.

Let's tackle this question piece by piece or use case by use case. If you add a smart contract into the Ethereum main net, then all you pay is the minimal fee to create the smart contract. When you send transactions to the smart contract, then you pay the transaction fee, amounting to a few cents. You don't have to pay a "mining" fee. Miners who are validating transactions and adding to blocks are rewarded by the network, and they also earn transaction fees.

With an application that writes thousands of smart contracts and millions of transactions, costs can be significant when adding up all smart contract and transaction fees. Then I am asked, as a follow-up question, "How do you deal with rising transaction costs?" I answer, "The same way we will deal with decreasing transaction costs," which is to either pass the cost to the users or absorb it as administrative/infrastructure cost.

All the foregoing rests on the assumption that you use public blockchains, for example, Ethereum, EOS, or NEM. No mining or transaction costs exist if you use a private network of Ethereum nodes or Hyperledger because the nodes are managed by a consortium, or a single entity, requiring zero economic incentive to mine blocks or to keep the transactions immutable.

Smart Contracts

Nick Szabo, in his seminal 1996 article, "Smart Contracts: Building Blocks for Digital Markets," proposed that *"…many kinds of contractual clauses (such as liens, bonding, delineation of property rights, etc.) can be embedded in the hardware and software in such a way as to make breach of contract expensive and prohibitive...*"[5] Fast forward to 2014, when Vitalik Buterin published a white paper on Ethereum as a platform to deploy next generation smart contracts, which Mr. Buterin described as "...cryptographic boxes that contain value and only unlock it if certain conditions are met..."[6]

The significance of Ethereum was, and still is, that it provides a blockchain-based platform to codify contracts with underlying cryptocurrency as a financial instrument for the network's security and governance. Ethereum embodied the concept of merging economics and cryptography just as Mr. Szabo theorized in his 1996 article. Other smart contract platforms on public blockchain include EOS, Stellar, and Cardano. Projects like Rootstock bring smart contract capability on the Bitcoin network. Corda and Hyperledger Fabric are widely used smart contract platforms for private blockchain infrastructure.

In simple terms, a smart contract is a piece of code that resides within the blockchain software, facilitating automatic transfer of assets between parties and contracts. Essentially, the code says to transfer a specific number of tokens from sender to receiver when a certain condition is met.

Since the code resides in blockchain, the terms of agreement between the parties are immutable, and the ledger keeps track of transactions created by the code. The smart contract provides authenticity and immutability of the logic embedded in the code, providing enforceability. Smart contracts also hold digital assets such as tokens. Based on the logic encoded in the smart contracts, they can move the tokens to other smart contracts or digital wallets when the contract terms hold true.[7]

---

[5]N. Szabo. 1996. "Smart Contracts: Building Blocks for Digital Markets." https://www.fon.hum.uva.nl/rob/Courses/InformationInSpeech/CDROM/Literature/LOT-winterschool2006/szabo.best.vwh.net/smart_contracts_2.html.

[6]V. Buterin. 2014. "Ethereum White Paper: Next Generation Smart Contract and Decentralized Application Platform," *Github*. https://github.com/ethereum/wiki/wiki/White-Paper.

[7]C. Dannen. 2017. *Introducing Ethereum and Solidity* (New York, NY: Apress).

The typical construct of an Ethereum-based smart contract is shown in Figure 3.6. Note that there are multiple iterations of smart contracts, depending on which blockchain infrastructure they reside on.

{Write contract code} -> Deploy in blockchain (Ethereum) -> Receive notification that contract code has been deployed along with a contract address -> Interact with the smart contract (input parameters) and pay gas fees -> Receive output or token

Figure 3.6 Simplified workflow of smart contract deployment in Ethereum

When smart contracts are deployed, they are officially added to the Ethereum blockchain, and anyone with the contract address can interact with the contract. Contracts can also be destroyed by the creator of the contract using a simple function. In that case, remaining tokens stored in the contract address are sent to a designated address, and the contract is deactivated.

Most prevalent smart contracts process monetary transactions between two parties. Some of the functions in a typical smart contract that receives fungible tokens, holds balances, or sends tokens utilize Ethereum Request for Comments (ERC-20) standards, shown in Figure 3.7.

totalSupply() returns the total supply of tokens the smart contract holds. It can hold zero balance.

balanceOf(address) returns the balance of tokens for a given address. This can be the address of the third-party sender or receiver.

transfer(address, unit) transfers tokens to a given address and returns true, as long as the person calling the function (msg.sender) has enough coins to send. It will also tell the network that the transfer has occurred by emitting details of the transfer.

Figure 3.7 Smart contracts can receive, hold, and send ERC-20 compatible tokens

The second type of smart contract does not involve monetary transactions but instead a transfer of assets from one participant to another, given the conditions mentioned in the logic are true. For example, Figure 3.8 shows transferring container ownership from shipper to carrier, or casting a vote for a legislation or a board member.

```
address public shipperAddress
address public carrierAddress
address public consigneeAddress
string containerID
Note: these addresses are public keys and not their names or physical address
containerTransfer(address from, address to, containerID) event will assign the
containerID from shipper's public address to carrier's address and record in the blockchain.
Similarly, the same function can transfer the container to a consignee, which, if successful,
the smart contract can transfer tokens from the initial supply to the carrier's address.
```

Figure 3.8 Smart contracts have addresses using which transactions are exchanged and stored

Obviously, the actual implementation of this smart contract is different depending on the type of coding environment and type of blockchain used such as Hyperledger or EOS. One of the strongest arguments for deploying smart contracts in a public blockchain like Ethereum or EOS is that once deployed, its public key is all that is needed to interact with the smart contract. The contract then becomes borderless and accessible to anyone, anywhere in the world.

Cryptocurrencies and Tokens

It wouldn't be a misprint to say that blockchain came into existence because of cryptocurrency which runs on blockchain. In recent days, two schools of thought have emerged. One school believes that without cryptocurrency adoption of blockchain is pointless. Another school believes that cryptocurrencies are a nuisance, or a Ponzi scheme; however, they insist that blockchain technology by itself is revolutionary.

Whatever school you belong to, let's talk about why cryptocurrencies exist in the first place. We'll also explore what happens when a permissionless blockchain application doesn't have a cryptocurrency. A section on Game Theory, which we'll dive into later, deals with the concept of economic incentives to keep the open network sustainable. Finally, we'll take a detour and describe the differences between a cryptocurrency and a token.

Besides being a financial instrument, cryptocurrencies are economic incentives for positive behavior by honest participants in each network.

Positive behavior is an integral part of a public, permissionless block-chain. Cryptocurrencies deter computational attacks by dishonest partici-pants by ensuring that honest network participants are rewarded without bias for their work in validating transactions and adding new blocks.

In Bitcoin, every 10 minutes, a block is added to the chain. The miner who can add that block to the network is rewarded with X amount of Bitcoin by the underlying protocol, otherwise known as block rewards. Adding blocks requires miners to expend resources for computation power. Without economic incentives, mining activities would be quite impossible to sustain. In many ways, blockchain users are paying for immutability and for peace of mind that comes from the thought that honest participants are keeping the underlying blockchain secure against block attacks.

From 2015 onward, we began to see the term "token" appear on the blockchain scene, and it is often used interchangeably with coin. Tokens are digital assets, or a type of cryptocurrency, that are built on top of an open blockchain that already has its own cryptocurrency. Hence, the term "coin" generally refers to any cryptocurrency that has its own separate, standalone blockchain.[8]

Tokens don't have their own blockchain but are built on existing in-frastructure such as Ethereum, Waves, and so forth using protocols such as ERC-20, ERC-721.[9] Tokens are also digital assets that support dApps, or decentralized applications.[10] The tokens have no inherent value by themselves but represent the value of utilization within the dApp or the project. Tokens that have specific use within the ecosystem of the under-lying applications are also called Utility Tokens. Tokens do not represent ownership of the company that is building the application and/or the entity that issued the token.

---

[8]D. Rhodes. August 10, 2018. "Crypto Coin vs. Token: Understanding the Differ-ence," *CoinCentral*. https://coincentral.com/crypto-coin-vs-token-cryptocurrency/.

[9]M. Cavichhioli. August 01, 2018. "The Difference between Token and Cryptocurrency," *Medium Corporation*. https://medium.com/novamining/the-difference-between-token-and-cryptocurrency-9dca9126fbda.

[10]StreamSpace. September 20, 2017. "Tokens vs Cryptocurrencies," *Medium Corporation*. https://medium.com/@stream_space/tokens-vs-cryptocurrencies-a22046202dc0.

Coins such as Bitcoin and Litecoin are typically capped, or fixed, with a small inflation factor associated as reward for maintenance of the blockchain. Unlike coins, organizations are not prevented from issuing more tokens, which could dilute the price of existing tokens already in circulation.

Why would anyone bother to create a token on an existing blockchain? Simple because it is easy to create one. In Ethereum, a smart contract can be used to define a token with a few lines of code. The smart contract essentially defines total supply of tokens and facilitates transactions to display who owns how many tokens. The disadvantage of creating a token on an existing blockchain is that the token relies on the network's underlying blockchain and hence on other teams that make regular technical improvements to the blockchain.

More tokens are being created today to represent physical and digital assets such as invoices, common stocks, debts, real estate, and storage space. We shall see more about this in later sections.

Merkle Trees

One of the fascinating concepts in blockchain is this: How can a miner verify transactions stored years ago without traversing hundreds of blocks down the blockchain? We know all the blocks are linearly and sequentially linked to one another. What does that mean? The answer lies in a data structure invented years before Bitcoin called a Merkle Tree.[11]

Figure 3.9 shows a simplified Merkle Tree. There are four unique hashes or digital fingerprints of four separate data blocks (they can consist of one or more individual transactions). In Merkle Tree nomenclature, these digital fingerprints are called leaf nodes. The first two hashes are then concatenated into a new hash (H1). The same operation is performed on the other two data blocks. Those two hashes (H1 and H2) are then concatenated and hashed again to create what is called a Root Hash (H3) or the Merkle root.

---

[11]R. Merkle. 1982. "Method of Providing Digital Signatures," United States, Patent No. US4309569A.

Root Hash/Merkle Root

H3=H(H1 + H2)

H1= (H(Data Block¹) + H(Data Block²))

H2 = (H(Data Block³) + H(Data Block⁴))

H(Data Block¹)   H(Data Block²)   H(Data Block³)   H(Data Block⁴)

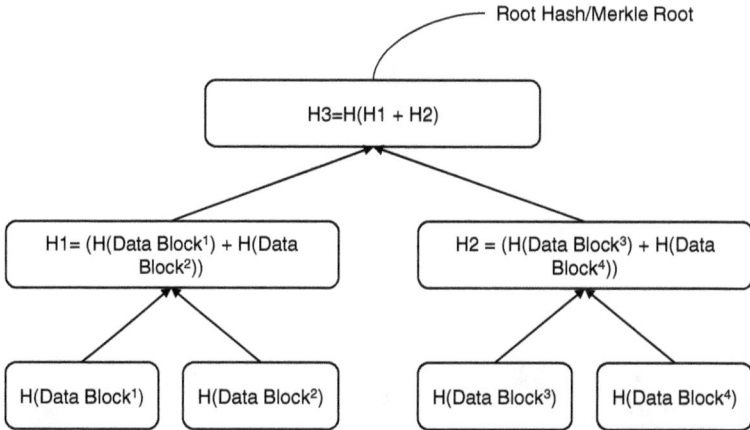

Figure 3.9 Structure of Merkle Tree with hashed data and Merkle Root

What is interesting about the foregoing tree is that the root hash is dependent on the hashes of the leaf nodes below it. If a transaction, or data block, is changed anywhere, then the root hash changes as well. Hence, Merkle Tree can show that no previous records have been altered. Also, Merkle Tree can be used to verify whether a specific transaction is included in the chain or not without querying down the blocks. Accomplishment of this task is carried out by ensuring that the hashes of the blocks are intact. Miners verify the presence of transactions and the chronological link between each block.

CHAPTER 4

Protocols and Concepts to Watch for

Protocols are rules and procedures that a system operates on. Networked systems are built on protocols that are agreed on by the participants as a precursor to participate. In the early days of blockchain, protocols meant consensus mechanisms—the rules and algorithms by which transactions were added in a block and how blocks were mined. Over the last few years, the definition of protocol has expanded to include privacy, smart contracts, interoperability, tokenization, and many more. These protocols manifested from the early days of blockchain to expand the use case of blockchain from financial transfer to other types of value transfers.

Protocols are the foundations of blockchain use cases. Hence, it is important for practitioners to keep an eye on revisions of existing protocols and emergence of new ones that might impact the systems you are attempting to build. Development of protocols is dynamic. In Ethereum and other public blockchain ecosystem, anybody can submit proposals to improve one or more underlying protocols. Such openness fosters rapid development, testing, and release of protocols. Nonetheless, I've briefly explained a few protocols and concepts that I think have significant importance in the adoption of blockchain technology in the future.

Zero-Knowledge Proofs

In our daily analog lives, when somebody asks you, "Are you a citizen or are you eligible to drive?" we whip out a passport or a driver's license. Although the person was only verifying your citizenship, you disclose more information than required—passport number, date of birth, etc. Zero-knowledge proof (ZKP) is a mathematical construct to prove to a verifier that a piece of information is correct without revealing details within the information.

Wikipedia has a great definition of ZKP:

"Zero-knowledge proof, or zero-knowledge protocol, is a method by which one party (the prover) can prove to another party (the verifier) that they know the value of x, without conveying any information apart from the fact that they know the value of x. The essence of zero-knowledge proofs is that it's trivial to prove one possesses knowledge of certain information by simply revealing it; the challenge is to prove such possession without revealing the information itself or any additional information."

We will not go into the details of the mathematical proof, which is quite complicated; however, zero-knowledge proofs have existed for over 20 years.

Here's a simple illustration of the concept.[1] Alice and Bob want to know if both are earning equal hourly wages without disclosing the actual amount. For simplicity, let's assume they are making $10, $20, $30, or $40 per hour.

1. Bob gets four lockable boxes and puts a label in each that says $10, $20, $30, and $40. All the boxes have separate keys.
2. Then Bob throws away all the keys except for the key to the box labeled $20.00 per hour (because he is making $20.00 per hour) and leaves with the key. When Alice sees the boxes later, she doesn't know which key Bob has with him.
3. Bob gives the locked boxes to Alice that have slits to insert pieces of paper. In private, Alice takes four small pieces of paper and writes "yes" on one of them and "no" on the others.
4. Remember, both are using the same set of boxes.
5. Alice slips paper with "yes" into the box labeled $30.00 per hour, because she makes $30.00 per hour, and slips the pieces of paper with

[1] C. Gidney. May 7, 2013. "Explain it like I'm Five: The Socialist Millionaire Problem and Secure Multi-Party Computation," *TwistedOakStudios*. http://twistedoakstudios .com/blog/Post3724_explain-it-like-im-five-the-socialist-millionaire-problem-and-secure-multi-party-computation.

"no" into the rest of the boxes and leaves. When Bob returns later, he doesn't know which box Alice slipped the pieces of paper into.

6. Bob returns and opens the one box he still has the key to—the one that is labeled $20.00 per hour—and sees the piece of paper with "no" written on it.

7. If it had been a "yes," it would mean Alice makes the same wage as Bob. Because the slip of paper says "no," it means that they have different wages.

8. We know that Bob makes $20.00 per hour and Alice makes $30.00 per hour. By opening the box and finding the piece of paper with a "no" on it, Bob learns that he and Alice have different wages, but he has no way of finding out the exact amount Alice makes. Alice may be making $10, $20, or $40 per hour.

9. Bob can show the piece of paper with "no" to Alice, and thus she will also know that their wages are different without disclosing the actual amount.

ZKP has evolved into zero-knowledge succinct non-interactive argument of knowledge (zk-SNARK) in the blockchain space to provide privacy and confidentiality of transactions in open blockchain. An algorithmic description of zk-SNARKs is provided here.[2] The most prominent blockchain-based systems using ZKPs are ZCash and Monero.[3]

In an open blockchain, when an asset is sent from one party to another, the details of that transaction are visible to every other party in the network. In such cases, zk-SNARKs can be used to prove that transactions are valid without revealing information about the sender, the receiver, and other details that can be stored off-chain. In verticals such as finance and trade finance, lack of privacy and confidentiality can be undesirable for end users.

---

[2]C. Lundkvist. March 27, 2017. "Introduction to zk-SNARKs with Examples," *Medium Corporation*. https://media.consensys.net/introduction-to-zksnarks-with-examples-3283b554fc3b.

[3]B. Curran. September 10, 2018. "What Are Zero-Knowledge Proofs? Complete Beginner's Guide," *Blockonomi*. https://blockonomi.com/zero-knowledge-proofs/.

Zk-SNARKs are also used in smart contracts[4] and can be used to prove that necessary steps or actions have been taken in the smart contract without revealing what they are. For example, smart contracts that release payment after proof of delivery or ownership transfer don't need to record details of proof of delivery in situations where confidentiality of such information is desired.

Instead of publishing the actual data on the blockchain, we can record mathematical proofs on the blockchain and prove to the smart contract that our transaction respects the business rules of the ecosystem without revealing the actual content of the transaction.[5] In our use case, we can change custody of an asset by sending a confidential message to another party. The party can then verify that the sender of the message is the actual custodian of the asset, using mathematical proof on the blockchain, as shown in Figure 4.1.

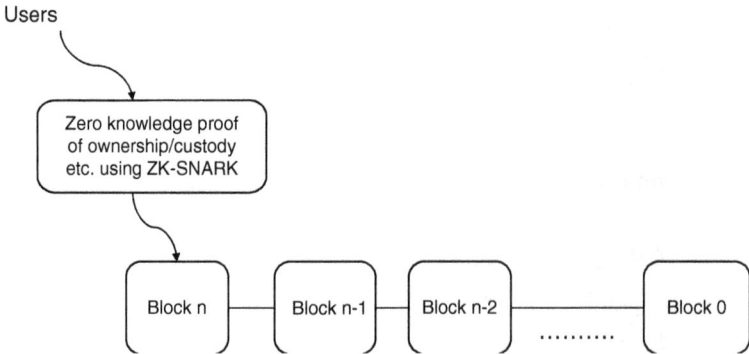

Figure 4.1 Users interact with blockchain using zk-SNARK protocols

If the proof is verified, the trading partner can complete the transfer by proving to the blockchain that he or she is the intended recipient of the transfer. That person is now the only custodian of the serial number

[4]S. Wurfel. September 6, 2018. "Zk-SNARKs Explained – Introduction to Privacy Protocol," *CaptainAltCoin*. https://captainaltcoin.com/zk-snarks-privacy/.
[5]M. Greco. April 10, 2018. "Does Proof of Existence Establish Provenance?", *Medium Corporation*. https://blog.chronicled.com/does-proof-of-existence-establish-provenance-5028fbd8c6da.

with the ability to generate a mathematical proof to demonstrate the new custody state and designate another trading partner to take ownership.

The zk-SNARK concept is also useful in tracking provenance of transactions between multiple parties without disclosing the entirety of those transactions. This is beneficial in moving high-value goods in complex supply chains such as pharmaceutical and ocean cargo movement. As physical goods and digital information about the goods move between stakeholders in the supply chain via smart contracts, confirmation of transactions and custody of goods can be proven to other parties without revealing the detailed information about the goods. This helps parties to maintain the confidentiality of information in public blockchain.

Identity to Interact with Blockchain Applications

A private key is a randomly generated 32-byte number that is unique to a user and should never be shared with others. A private key is used to generate a public key. A public address is a hashed version of the public key. Public addresses are like our bank account information. We provide public addresses to other parties to send or receive cryptocurrencies and other relevant data.

In public blockchain, there are no usernames or passwords. Identity is simply to create your own private/public key and use those key pairs to authenticate transactions in the smart contract or cryptocurrency transfer. Government-issued identities are not required to send bitcoins or Ether, or to interact with smart contracts on the Ethereum network or other public blockchain infrastructure. The combination of private and public keys is enough for blockchain nodes to verify transactions as described in the earlier chapter. When users are not required to show government-issued identifications, they can use applications like MetaMask or uPort to create private and public keys to interact with smart contracts and dApps.

For dApps and other applications that need government-issued identity verification, third-party decentralized identity solutions are available. Examples include ShoCard, Civic, BitID, and ID.me. These services perform identity proofing of users on the basis of existing trusted credentials, such as a passport or driver's license. The service will then record identity attestations on a blockchain for later validation by identity requesters, preventing direct storage of government-issued identity by the dApp and application developers. The concept of "self-sovereign identity" is getting much attention because of the spread of private information leaks.

Three kinds of identity architectures exist today:

Centralized Trusted Identity—A traditional identity model by which an identity is owned and controlled by an application provider. Users rely on the provider to create and manage identities with the possibility that their identities can be taken away. In the case of Federated Identity, applications can use single sign-on procedures provided by Google, Facebook, LinkedIn, for example.

Self-sovereign Identity—An identity that is owned and controlled by its owner, or user, without the need to rely on external administrative authority or the possibility that this identity can be taken away. Self-sovereign identity can be enabled by a decentralized identity ecosystem that facilitates the recording and exchange of identity attributes as well as the propagation of trust among participating entities. Examples include Sovrin, uPort, and OneName, to name a few. Self-sovereign identity is like the current model of transacting on Ethereum or Bitcoin, in which anyone can create a public and private key without attestation or revoking authority from a centralized institution.

In general, self-sovereign identity works by anchoring identity, issued by government or other agencies, into a public blockchain. The issuer, in this case the government, submits a claim that an identity for the user exists. The user holds the identity, like a card without personally identifiable information, and countersigns the claim using blockchain. A verifier simply needs to check the existence of the claim in the public blockchain. The verifier, in this case, can be a website. Using the identity anchored in blockchain, users can register or sign in on websites without adding personal information such as date of birth, social security number, or age verification.

Decentralized Trusted Identity—An identity that is provided by a centralized service, performing identity proofing of users based on existing trusted credentials, such as a passport or driver's license, and records identity attestations on a blockchain for later validation by third parties. Figure 4.2 shows a flow of data requests in this identity model that leverages identity provided by trusted entities such as governments.

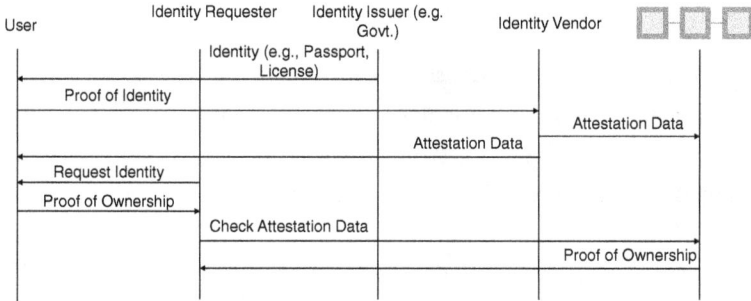

Figure 4.2 Decentralized trusted identity that leverages government-issued identity

Examples include ShoCard, CIVIC, BitID, ID.me, and IDchainZ. Decentralized trusted identity is a compromise between the traditional model and the self-sovereign model with a specific realization. Self-sovereign identity is unsuitable for applications that need attestation of government-issued identity, but it does allow the user to create boundaries regarding who uses the identity and in what manner. Decentralized trusted identity is used to prove relationships between individuals within varying companies.

Companies like ShoCard provide a trusted identity that leverages blockchain to bind a user identifier, an existing trusted credential such as a passport or driver's license, and additional identity attributes together via cryptographic hashes stored in blockchain. The technique uses public blockchain, like Bitcoin, as a time-stamping service for signing cryptographic hashes of the user's government-provided or employer-provided identity information. The provider, ShoCard, incorporates a central server as an essential part of its scheme that intermediates the exchange of encrypted identity information between a user and a relying party.

Decentralized trusted identity is a compromise between the traditional model, usernames and passwords, and public and private key identity. Public and private key pairs used as an identity are not suitable for applications that require attestation of government-issued identity. Decentralized trusted identity is also used to prove relationships between individuals with companies. Only those individuals can log into applications. It will also fulfill Know Your Customer (KYC) requirements, because trusted credentials are part of the identity.

Stable Cryptocurrencies

Cryptocurrencies are notoriously volatile, at least for the time being. Analyzing reasons for volatility is not within the scope of this book. Businesses desiring to transact in cryptocurrencies run the risk of instant price appreciation or depreciation during the time invoices are received and settled. The only way around this is to settle those transactions immediately and convert to much more stable currency.

Volatility puts a significant burden on businesses to report price appreciation and subject to capital gains taxes or depreciation and report losses in the United States and other countries. When businesses settle invoices or purchases instantly, the risk of volatility may not be that high. However, many other businesses settle invoices in weeks or even months. In that situation, both receivers and payers will be faced with the predicament of not knowing how much they will pay or receive.

Stable coins work around the volatility issue and are designed to be stable by pegging to local fiat currency. Stable coins are simply cryptocurrencies with stable value. The general theory is that fiat currencies fluctuate less than cryptocurrencies and hence pegged stable coins may have more traction among businesses and even individuals who seek stable payment mechanisms. They share most of the features that make Bitcoin and other cryptocurrencies so appealing, yet don't suffer from the same volatility, making them more usable as a medium of exchange and account.[6] According to a report titled "State of Stable Coins," there are 23 stable coins in circulation at the time of this writing.[7] Stable coins generally fall within these three categories[8]:

Off-chain asset backed—In this model, tokens are "backed" by local fiat in reserve based on 1 to 1 issuance. Stable coin issuers must demonstrate to the public through audits or attestations that they do have

---

[6]K. Samani. January 17, 2018. "An Overview of Stable Coins," *Multicoin Capital.* https://multicoin.capital/2018/01/17/an-overview-of-stablecoins/.

[7]"State of Stable Coins," *Blockchain.com.* https://www.blockchain.com/ru/static/pdf/StablecoinsReportFinal.pdf, (accessed December 20, 2019).

[8]B. Memon. "Guide to Stable Coin: Types of Stable Coins and Its Importance," *Masterthecrypto.* https://masterthecrypto.com/guide-to-stablecoin-types-of-stablecoins/, (accessed November 21, 2018).

adequate collateral amount, in this case fiat, in reserve to guarantee that every token issued is backed by the same amount of fiat. This model is easy to understand for consumers. However, the issuer needs to hold very large, auditable amounts in reserve and to find ways to generate revenue instead of letting it sit in a bank account.

Crypto-asset backed—Tokens are minted in smart contracts by locking high-value cryptocurrencies such as Ether and Bitcoin as collaterals. Users then receive the stable coin as a loan. Once the loan is paid off, the locked cryptocurrency is released back to the user. To de-risk against volatility of cryptocurrencies, stable coins are often overcollateralized when borrowing loans. The price of a stable coin is algorithmically, and to some extent manually, adjusted by the market's supply and demand of the stable coin. Most stable coin projects in this category are currently built on top of the public Ethereum network.[9]

Algorithmic central bank or seigniorage shares—Using smart contracts, tokens are automatically issued on the basis of their peg with fiat. Like a central bank, the smart contract issues new tokens if the price of the stable coin is high and burns if the price is too low. This type of stable coin is not common; one of the reasons for this may be that it also involves issuance of bonds that are deemed securities in many jurisdictions.

Stable coins have yet to be ubiquitous in small business transactions and yet to step into large financial transactions such as trade finance and cross-border payments. I believe this is because of several hindrances—regulatory and tax issues, user experience, and liquidity markets.

Protocols to Implement NFTs

We talked about nonfungible assets in the earlier chapter—physical assets, invoices, music rights, and so forth. Among the many innovative, and perhaps game-changing, benefits of blockchain is the creation of digital tokens representing physical assets. These tokens are called nonfungible

---

[9]Price Waters Cooper. October 2018. "Stable Coin Evolution and Market Trends," *Price Waters Cooper*. https://www.pwc.com.au/pdf/stable-coin-evolution-and-market-trends.pdf.

tokens (NFT), which are unique representations of an asset in the form of a token. Once a digital representation of an asset is created and recorded in blockchain, the token holder can sell and transfer the asset on block-chain to anyone else and, in that process, digitally splice the asset into multiple pieces.

ERC-721 is a free, open standard that defines the minimum interface a smart contract must implement to allow unique tokens to be managed, owned, and traded. It does not mandate a standard for token metadata or restrict adding supplemental functions. ERC-721 describes how to build nonfungible or unique tokens on the Ethereum blockchain. Since each ERC-721 token is unique,[10] they are referenced on the blockchain by a unique identification.

The protocol allows on-chain registries to store immutable provenance of asset ownership in case the asset is transferred to another owner(s). The holder of an asset on blockchain is provided a way to prove that the asset belongs to the token holder using private and public keys. An asset's at-tributes may be stored in an off-chain database to preserve confidentiality. When an asset is transferred owing to liquidity, the blockchain records the transfer, the token owned by the debtor is destroyed in the smart con-tract, and a new token is created and provided to a creditor.

I'll talk about ERC-721 protocol in more detail in Chapter 8 when discussing tokenization of nonfungible assets.

ERC-998 is an extension to the ERC-721 standard that adds the abil-ity for NFTs to own other NFTs and ERC-20 tokens.[11] The protocol allows for the creation of composable NFTs. ERC-721 is used to refer to the "parent" asset, while its composable "children" assets will refer to the ERC-721 or the ERC-20 tokens owned by them.[12] The standard also allows for strict mapping of the relationship between parent and child to-kens, as shown in Figure 4.3. Child tokens are only able to be transferred from the contract if the sender also owns the parent token identification.

[10]"ERC-721," http://erc721.org, (accessed December 22, 2018).
[11]"Composable Non-Fungible Token Standard," http://erc998.org, (accessed Decem-ber 19, 2019).
[12]M. Lockyer. April 14, 2018. "Introducing Crypto Composables," *Medium Corporation*. https://medium.com/coinmonks/introducing-crypto-composables-ee5701fde217.

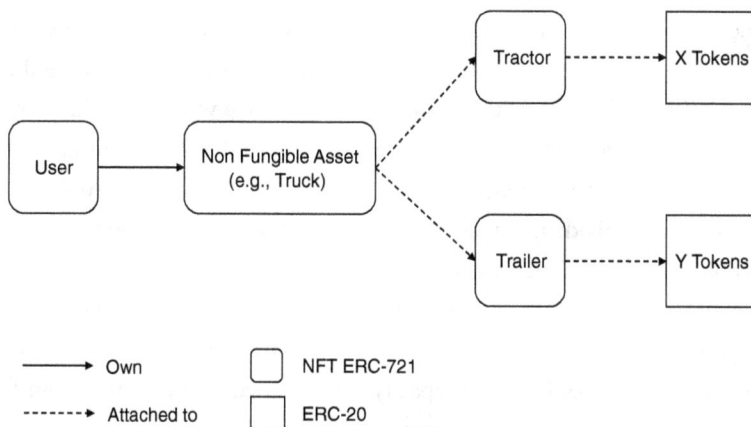

Figure 4.3 Parent nonfungible token represented by child tokens

Source: Recreated from Lockeyer and Mudge.[13]

Layer 2 Protocols and Scalability

Consider the following thought for a moment. Can people use 18-wheeler trucks to deliver a small parcel? Sure, but it is not cost effective. Eighteen-wheelers are designed to carry large parcels, or pallets, which are then broken down into small parcels at a warehouse. From there, those small pallets are carried by a motorbike or a small van and delivered to your home. Layer 2 solutions are like small vans. Can you imagine 18-wheelers delivering small parcels everywhere? It would be slow, clunky, and expensive. That business model would not scale.

The main purpose of Layer 2 solutions is to scale blockchain transaction capacity. Sending microtransactions using Bitcoin or Ethereum's main blockchain is slow, clunky, and expensive. Hence, such transactions are exchanged within the upper layer without directly issuing transactions on the main chain, otherwise known as Layer 1.

One example of Layer 2 is the Lightning Network solution built on top of Bitcoin.[14] The general idea is that if you must make small payments with

---

[13]M. Luckeyer and N. Mudge. April 15, 2018. "ERC-998 Composable Non-Fungible Token Standard #998," *GitHub*. https://github.com/ethereum/eips/issues/998.

[14]"Lightning Network: Scalable, Instant Bitcoin/Blockchain Transactions," *Lightning Network*, https://lightning.network, (accessed January 11, 2019).

another party, both parties agree to create a multiparty address using a smart contract, opening a channel between both parties. Parties transact using this smart contract and close the channel whenever they wish. Individual payments in the channel are not sent to the Bitcoin blockchain for confirmations. Only the final balance is then broadcast to the main network, or Layer 1.

Because individual transactions do not need block confirmations, transactions are quick. Hence, Lightning Network can be used at retail point-of-sale terminals, with user device-to-device transactions, or anywhere instant payments are needed. Since January 2018, the number of channels has grown from 0 to 24,000, and capacity has increased to over 600 Bitcoin.[15]

Neha Narula, of Massachusetts Institute of Technology, says, "A defining feature of Layer 2 is that computation is moved off-chain, either to enable privacy or to save computing resources.[16] Rather than having the script of a program executed by every computer in the blockchain network, "[i]t is implemented simply by two or more computers involved in the transaction." Ms. Narula further says, "You get similar security protections to on-chain transactions because the blockchain acts as the anchor of trust."

Another example is a concept called sidechains, where a separate blockchain, with a "bridge" to Layer 1, transfers assets back and forth between the two layers. Figure 4.4 shows Layer 2 blockchain writing blocks of hashed transactions to Bitcoin's blockchain. Block headers, hash, from the sidechain's blockchain are periodically sent to Layer 1 to leverage the security of the Layer 1 blockchain.

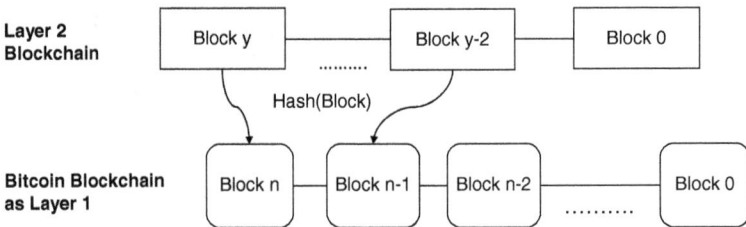

Figure 4.4 Layer 2 blockchain or sidechain adding hashed transactions to Bitcoin blockchain

---

[15]"Real-Time Lightning Network Statistics," https://1ml.com/statistics.

[16]M. Casey. May 30, 2018. "Layer 2 Blockchain Tech Is an Even Bigger Deal Than You Think," *CoinDesk*. https://www.coindesk.com/layer-2-blockchain-tech-even-bigger-deal-think.

Sidechains were first proposed by Back in an article titled "Enabling Blockchain Innovations with Pegged Sidechains."[17] In their article, pegged sidechains are defined as a technology that enables Bitcoin and other assets to be transferred between multiple blockchains.

Create a transaction on the first blockchain, or parent chain, locking the assets. Create a transaction on the second blockchain, or sidechain, whose inputs contain a cryptographic proof that the lock was done correctly. A corresponding amount of coins is released on the sidechain. The user is then able to spend the coins on the sidechain. When moving the asset from the sidechain to the parent chain, the user sends the coins from the sidechain to an output address, where they are locked.

In business applications, storing transactions on the main layer might be slow and expensive. Assuming the sidechain is relatively faster than Layer 1, using the upper layer for smart contracts and transactions makes operational sense. Using Bitcoin or Ethereum to store hash from Layer 2 provides additional security and saves on Layer 1 transaction fees.

A sidechain is a separate blockchain that is attached to its parent blockchain using a two-way peg.[18] The two-way peg enables interchangeability of assets at a predetermined rate between the parent blockchain and the sidechain. Two-way peg refers to the mechanism by which coins are transferred between the sidechain and the parent chain and back at a fixed or otherwise deterministic exchange rate.

An obvious benefit of sidechains is to create innovative asset classes on a separate blockchain that uses a more secure parent chain such as Bitcoin or Ethereum to maintain security of assets. Sidechains are independent of parent chains in terms of blockchain operation.

Smart Contracts are Judges; Oracles are Attorneys

Smart contracts were designed to be lightweight, computationally speaking, so that transactions can be confirmed quickly without putting a

---

[17]A. Back. October 22, 2014. "Blockchain Innovations with Pegged Sidechains," *Blockstream*. https://blockstream.com/sidechains.pdf.
[18]S. Ray. January 22, 2018. "What are Sidechains?", *Hackernoon*. https://hackernoon.com/what-are-sidechains-1c45ea2daf3.

heavy burden on the blockchain infrastructure. The best use of smart contracts is to transfer assets and currencies between counterparty addresses if certain conditions hold true.

Transferring balances between counterparties is easy. The tricky part comes with verifying whether the condition triggering the balance transfer is reliable or not. Oracles are external programs that provide real-world conditional data as input into a smart contract. Examples of external data include current temperature, price of gold in mercantile exchange at 9:00AM CST, proof of payment, and proof of delivery.

It is important to note that oracles are not the source of such data. They are merely the vehicles that provide data to smart contracts. Figure 4.5 shows oracle service in between external data sources (e.g., market information, websites) and smart contracts. The burden of computation to acquire data is on the oracles and not on the smart contract itself.

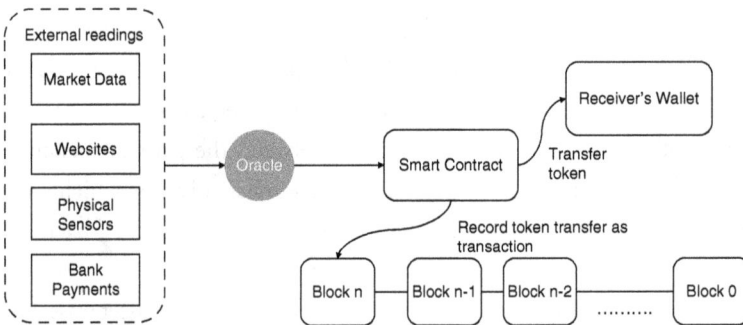

Figure 4.5 Oracle services provide inputs to smart contracts from external sources

When smart contracts first appeared, their inability to connect to outside information sources such as URLs and data sources quickly became an issue for their practical application.

The issue was aptly labeled "Oracle problem." In theory, the reliance of smart contracts on centralized data sources seems counterintuitive.[19] However, in practice, we must rely on outside sources. It's a bit difficult to

[19]M. Orcutt. November 19, 2018. "Blockchain Smart Contracts are Finally Good for Something in the Real World," *MIT Technology Review.*

imagine that every data source will be validated by multiple independent entities. So is the oracle problem really a problem?[20]

Nonetheless, let's talk about a major issue with oracle utilization, which is ensuring the reliability of the data source. It can be solved using decentralized oracles, in which multiple nodes arrive at consensus independently. For example, a majority among 10 nodes independently verify that the current temperature in Alaska is 60 degrees Fahrenheit. If we label these nodes as "independent validators," a small number can collude to deliberately falsify data entering smart contracts.

Business operations receive data from sources that are private and are publicly unavailable for multiple nodes and independent entities to validate; for example, truck telematics position, field sensor information, and patient health information. One way to ensure tamperproofing is by the sending device signing the data with a private/public key. The data is then verified by the smart contract or the oracle using the sender's public key.

Cross-Chain Interoperability

A lot of buzz has surfaced around the need for blockchain interoperability to help serve different industries. Industries such as logistics and supply chain will use a wide array of applications built on open, enterprise blockchain to trade, share, and swap assets. In an interoperable world, users in multiple blockchains can transfer and verify information about assets with little effort.

The value proposition for interoperability between blockchains is clear and significant. It will lower the entry cost to develop applications compatible between systems to the benefit of end users. Let's look at use cases that blockchain interoperability should support as well as potential strategies. By no means is this an exhaustive list of use cases and solutions.

Use Case 1—Trading or swapping assets between different blockchains

---

[20]A. Tsankov. June 21, 2018. "The 'Oracle Problem' isn't a Problem, and Why Smart Contracts Make Insurance Better for Everyone," *Medium Corporation*. https://medium .com/@antsankov/the-oracle-problem-isnt-a-problem-and-why-smart-contracts-makes-insurance-better-for-everyone-8c979f09851c.

Alice has X asset in Blockchain A and Bob has Y asset in Blockchain B. If they want to swap each other's asset, then both Alice and Bob must use a trusted intermediary or a notary. If both Blockchain A and B were interoperable, Alice and Bob would be able to trade each other's assets (a process known as a cross-chain swap) without a trusted intermediary. Swapping assets, especially tokens across chains, requires using the in-house ledger of centralized exchanges and then withdrawing the new token on a new chain. This process is expensive because both Alice and Bob will have to pay transaction fees to the intermediary. Swapping and trading assets is common in bulk logistics and maritime. The ownership of shipments on the way from New York to Hamburg may be traded and swapped many times. If we are to disrupt the industry by tokenizing physical assets on smart contracts, then interoperability is critical for frictionless trading and liquidity.

Use Case 2—Communication between blockchains to verify each other's transactions

Alice has ownership of a container full of auto parts. The ownership is registered in a private blockchain application (it can be public as well.) The container is transported and delivered to Bob, who is an auto manufacturer. Alice registers Bob as the new owner of the container. Bob's blockchain needs to verify that Alice's blockchain has confirmed that the container ownership has been changed to him. Alice's blockchain needs to do the same on her end. An auto manufacturer like Bob receives parts and orders from hundreds of suppliers spread across the globe. How realistic is it to think that Bob and all his suppliers, who may also supply to other manufacturers, will be on the same blockchain that Alice uses?

Vitalik Buterin, in "Chain Interoperability," mentioned two other use cases that garnered attention because of their usability in the supply chain. They are combined and summarized next as Use Case 3.

Use Case 3—Portability and encumbrance of invoices

Alice, the carrier, has an invoice anchored in Ethereum and wants to borrow against it from a bank. The bank agrees to provide finance against the invoice, but its smart contract that is in a different blockchain needs to lock the invoice in Ethereum so that Alice doesn't go to another bank with the same invoice and double spend it. If not utilized on another chain, then the asset can be moved back to the original chain. Also, the asset in the original chain can be locked by another chain to finance it as a collateral. Multiple parties "sharing" a blockchain would reduce the likelihood of fraud in invoices and other trade documents.

Trusted notary mechanism—One obvious solution is to utilize a trusted intermediary that listens to events such as Alice and Bob's transactions in both or multiple blockchains, providing digital signature of proofs that those transactions have taken place. Mr. Buterin calls it a "notary mechanism." An obvious flaw, or rather shortcoming, in this approach is the centralized intermediary, which can be improved by creating a decentralized exchange, which would then become a custodian to maintain a proof that an asset transfer has taken place.

Hash lock time contracts—Hash lock time contracts do not require knowledge of what's happening in the counterparty's blockchain. These contracts remove the requirement of notaries and transfer tokens after a condition encoded in the smart contract is satisfied. Hash lock time contracts are enforced by the blockchain where the parties transacting only need to trust the blockchain to correctly execute the contract. It also works well in a payment channel environment. The simplest description of hash lock time contract, as described by Mr. Buterin in "Chain Interoperability" is as follows:

1. Alice generates a random secret, s, and computes the hash of the secret, $hash(s) = h$. Alice sends the hash, h, to Bob.
2. Alice and Bob both lock their assets into a smart contract with the following rules. First off, Alice locks first, Bob locks after seeing Alice's asset successfully locked. On Alice's side, if the secret is provided within a certain time frame, then the token is transferred to Bob; otherwise, it is sent back to Alice. On Bob's side, if the correct secret, or the value whose hash is h, is provided, then the token is transferred to Alice; otherwise, it is sent back to Bob.
3. Alice reveals the secret to claim the token from Bob's contract. However, this ensures that Bob learns the secret, allowing him to claim the asset from Alice's smart contract.

Cross-chain message relay—Instead of relying on a trusted intermediary to pass information between the two blockchains, one of the blockchains, let's say Blockchain A, takes the block header of Blockchain B to verify transactions and confirm an event or state in Blockchain A. However, this is more nuanced than it sounds, because both blockchains need to use a similar consensus mechanism and structure of ledger. Fahad Shah described cross-chain messaging as basically a query of belief.[21] Mr. Shah questioned how one can design a system to relay messages between blockchains in a situation where one of the chains may be an orphan or forked. It is also conceivable that a message being sent is from a forked or orphan chain.

There are at least a dozen projects in this space attacking the problem of interoperability from multiple angles. For example, Cosmos Network is a project that is creating a hub that connects independent blockchains, called *zones*.[22] Interoperability standards between blockchains will be a long and grueling game because, at present, the market's focus is to increase the adoption of blockchain applications. However, in the absence of clear interoperable solutions and standards, innovations in interorganizational tokenization, asset trading, and invoice financing will hit a brick wall.

Game-Theoretic Network Incentives

Game theory is the systematic study of strategic interactions among rational individuals. It is the process of modeling strategic interactions between two or more players in a situation containing a set of rules and outcomes.[23] Game theory is used in several disciplines but most notably as a tool within the study of economics. Most of us know game theory from the movie *Beautiful Mind*, which portrays the life and discoveries of mathematician John Nash, played by Russell Crowe.

Use of game theory in the context of blockchain is quite interesting in that all the classical components in a game are available in blockchain, especially open and permissionless blockchain. Miners play the following key roles in blockchain:

[21]K. Samani. January 27, 2018. "The Opportunity for Interoperable Chains of Chains," *Coindesk*. https://www.coindesk.com/opportunity-interoperable-chains-chains.
[22]"What is Cosmos?", *Tendermint Inc.*, https://cosmos.network/intro.
[23]D. McNulty. November 13, 2019. "The Basics of Game Theory," *Investopedia*. https://www.investopedia.com/articles/financial-theory/08/game-theory-basics.asp.

- Miners are the players who participate in the game. They are also strategic decision makers in validating transactions and creating a correct chain.
- Miners use multiple computational strategies, such as acquisition of hash power and automation to mine one crypto versus another based on market prices and difficulty rates.
- Miners are awarded with a diminishing rate of coins for their efforts in validating transactions and adding them to a block.
- At a given point in time, miners are presented with the current state of blocks, difficulty, coin market prices, and the new block being proposed because of new transactions.
- The resulting blockchain is always the longest chain with valid transactions. Underlying protocol and economic incentives encourage miners to stay within the boundaries of the protocol. Steep costs are involved if one attempts to tamper with transactions such as failure to receive block rewards.

Mathew Finestone wrote in *Game Theory and Blockchain*, "The goal of game theory for cryptocurrency is to model human reasoning to build networks that need no oversight yet have positive outcomes for the greater good. Unfortunately, planning for unpredictable human decisions first requires that we understand what motivates people, which is easier said than done."[24] In open blockchain, finding what motivates people is difficult to predict.

Hopefully, all the miners are economically motivated to keep the mining operation running. However, price collapse of the cryptocurrency may negatively challenge the motivation. We've also seen cases where certain groups of miners refused to participate in a hard fork (references) or other cases where they forced hard forks owing to disagreements in long-term sustainability of the cryptocurrency.

Miners have a lot of power in the blockchain system, and if they do choose to cheat for their own personal gain, they can force the community to choose a different chain. To mitigate that, the blockchain uses game theory mechanics to keep the system sustainable in the sense that it

---

[24]M. Finestone. January 5, 2018. "Game Theory and Blockchain," *Medium Corporation*. https://medium.com/@matthewfinestone/game-theory-and-blockchain-db46e67933d7.

is difficult for a single miner to force a new chain, even if the miner possesses over 51 percent hash power.

Mr. Buterin wrote in a Medium post, "... Because proof of work security can only come from block rewards, and incentives to miners can only come from the risk of them losing their future block rewards, proof of work necessarily operates on the logic of massive power incentivized into existence by massive rewards."[25] However, one specific concern has been concentration of hash power among a handful of mining pools. At the time of this writing, four of the largest mining pools control over 50 percent of the total hash power in Bitcoin, 3 pools in the case of Ethereum.[26]

Mr. Buterin further wrote, "Proof of stake breaks this symmetry by relying not on rewards for security, but rather penalties." In a future version of Ethereum integrating proof of stake, validators, instead of miners, hold funds as stake and are rewarded for locking up their capital and maintaining nodes. Hence, in comparison with proof of work type consensus, security is achieved by penalizing validators rather than relying on block rewards distributed to miners.

Other blockchain protocols, such as EOS, use a Delegated Proof of Stake consensus mechanism by allowing users to vote on delegates, or block producers. Delegates are the trusted parties responsible for maintaining the network. There are a handful of such producers, and rumors of collusion between producers surfaced in October 2018, rattling the EOS community.[27] Even before that, "centralization" and overreach of block producers to freeze accounts of users has been thrown into question.[28]

---

[25]V. Buterin. December 30, 2016. "A Proof of Stake Design Philosophy," *Medium Corporation.* https://medium.com/@VitalikButerin/a-proof-of-stake-design-philosophy-506585978d51.

[26]J. Hagermann. May 12, 2018. "Proof of Stake (Casper Ethereum) Explained," *Medium Corporation.* https://medium.com/@johanneshage97/proof-of-stake-casper-ethereum-explained-682d663440d5.

[27]A. Berman. October 2, 2018. "EOS Developer Acknowledges Claims of Collusion and Mutual Voting Between Nodes," *CoinTelegraph.* https://cointelegraph.com/news/eos-developer-acknowledges-claims-of-collusion-and-mutual-voting-between-nodes.

[28]S. Miah. July 6, 2018. "EOS: Trouble on the Horizon? State of Current Governance Explained," *Medium Corporation.* https://medium.com/datadriveninvestor/eos-trouble-on-the-horizon-state-of-current-governance-explained-4b4f16bd6a41.

CHAPTER 5

Private versus Public versus Consortium Blockchains

The subject of a perpetual debate is why public blockchain is a terrible idea because it is slow and cannot confirm so many transactions per second. Another side of the debate is that the private blockchain is nothing but a glorified database. Therefore, consortium blockchain is a compromise between the two. These debates are based on technical attributes distinguishing between the three blockchain types.

In addition to their technical dissimilarities, you should know why one is more suitable than the other for the application or use case one is intending to construct. The thought process here is that a thorough business case and pain points analysis should be used to define which style of blockchain to implement. Otherwise, you might be better off with a centralized database.

Private Blockchains

In simple terms, private blockchain restricts access to its network of nodes and decides who can view and transact within the network. Access control is the biggest differentiator between private blockchain and public ones. Access to blockchain is restricted to certain individuals or entities, and mining is performed on a limited set of nodes. As shown in Figure 5.1, there may be one or more validator nodes. Hence, the deployment footprint is small compared with a public blockchain.

Private blockchain is not decentralized from the viewpoint of both participation and governance. Also, mining rewards are not necessary because the network is controlled and managed by a single trusted entity or authority. Mining to reach consensus only guarantees to the participants that transactions have not been tampered with.

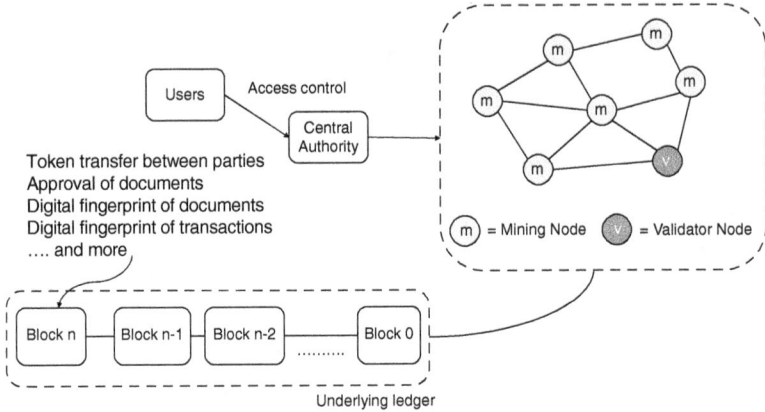

Figure 5.1 Limited number of mining and validator nodes with access to white-listed participants

Use of private blockchains gained traction because of the needs of enterprises. They expressed the need to manage access to transactions and the underlying ledger. We have seen many implementations of private blockchains in which one company tells its vendors and subcontractors that they must submit transactions to an application running on private blockchain in order to achieve some objectives such as provenance and traceability.

Public versus Private Blockchains

In a public blockchain, anyone can read and add transactions if they are valid against the underlying protocols. In addition, anyone can participate in the consensus process of determining what blocks get added to the chain. Hence, these blockchains are global, decentralized, and censorship resistant. Also, there is less expectation of confidentiality with public blockchain.

Private blockchains then entered the scene, reading and adding transactions to an underlying ledger performed by a single entity.[1] Hence, that entity can alter transactions without requiring consensus with others who are participating in reading and writing transactions.

---

[1]V. Buterin. August 6, 2015. "On Public and Private Blockchains," *Ethereum Blog.* https://blog.ethereum.org/2015/08/07/on-public-and-private-blockchains/.

Benefits of private blockchain are speed of transactions and higher levels of confidentiality because it doesn't require consensus between multiple independent nodes. A primary weakness is that there are also no validator or mining nodes.[2] Speed of transactions is higher compared with public blockchain because a small number of nodes is enough to maintain the state of the ledger. Another benefit that proponents of private blockchains promote is that they provide privacy, unlike public blockchains. On the other hand, it is not privacy that is the question, but rather *permissions* to read and write transactions. Public blockchains do not necessarily reveal confidential information but, rather, who added the transaction and who transacted with whom.

Blockchain maximalists argue that private blockchains are nothing but a glorified database with cryptography because an implementing agency can dictate the terms of using the system and, in some cases, force other participants to use it. For example, a large retailer requires its vendors to use the system if they want to remain a vendor. It can be easily argued, "Why does the retailer need a blockchain instead of a centralized database?" Hence, a need for blockchain for this kind of vertical collaboration is questionable.

Debate about the Private Blockchain

Enterprise communities, especially IBM and banks, have been pioneering the adoption of private blockchain in a variety of use cases through well-known proof of concepts. Private blockchains are often presented as an alternative to public blockchain for enterprise use cases that require access, control, and privacy. Truths are revealed, but so are misconceptions because private blockchains by themselves do not have privacy built in.

Privacy is added to it using access control, by which only individuals with proper credentials can see the transactions added to blocks that are typically deployed in a controlled cloud server environment. But once somebody gets into the system and because there are a small number of

[2]Hackernoon. August 1, 2018. "Blockchain Architecture Analysis: Private vs Public vs Consortium," *Hackernoon.* https://hackernoon.com/blockchain-architecture-analysis-private-vs-public-vs-consortium-65eb061b907b.

nodes, tamper resistance of the private blockchain can be very quickly compromised. In a use case where a private blockchain is being shared with multiple known and trusted parties, you wouldn't put information sensitive to your organization or to individuals in the organization. The same applies to public blockchain. Instead, sensitive information is stored off-chain.

The other argument presented about private blockchain's benefits over public blockchain is transaction throughput or transactions per second (TPS). Yes, it is obvious that private blockchains can process more TPS because their mining, or census, process is faster owing to the small number of nodes and "miner" nodes that do not compete for block rewards.

High TPS is a requirement for use cases with high-frequency transaction processing such as real-time stock trades. However, there are use cases that do not require a high TPS, such as real-estate transfers and international supply chains, where transaction settlements that take minutes or hours to complete are acceptable.

Use of private blockchain for vertical collaboration use cases is weak. For example, you are a big company that buys billions of dollars worth of auto parts from dozens of independent vendors, and you want to ensure parts can be tracked and traced for provenance, recalls, and so forth. You go and tell all your vendors they must use this new system on private blockchain. What is the merit of using blockchain in this environment other than a centralized cloud database? You've already forced your suppliers to use it. The vendors must trust that you will not tamper with the ledger (Figure 5.2).

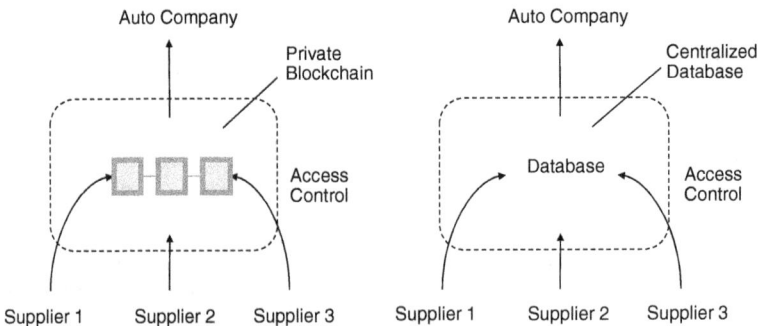

Figure 5.2 Centralized database versus private blockchain

In this example, the blockchain that you own, deploy, and maintain is no different than a trusted central database. The blockchain, in this case, cannot function as a trust layer when suppliers are forced to trust; otherwise they'll lose business.

Hence, private blockchains are much inferior to public blockchain when it comes to security, tamper-proofing, and censorship resistance. They are certainly not decentralized. Some have even argued that private blockchains are nothing but glorified, distributed databases. I wouldn't go that far, but it certainly has a strong use case for consortium-type blockchain in which peers must share the database containing strong access control.

Here Comes Consortium Blockchain

Multiple companies can form a consortium with a common purpose. Among those purposes are interbank fraud prevention, threat intelligence, and asset sharing, implementing a platform with a ledger deployed on several nodes with equal access to the consortium members. The ledger is fully transparent within the consortium members and can even maintain nodes with implementation of byzantine fault tolerance. Figure 5.3 shows members with access to a blockchain maintained and operated exclusively on behalf of the members.

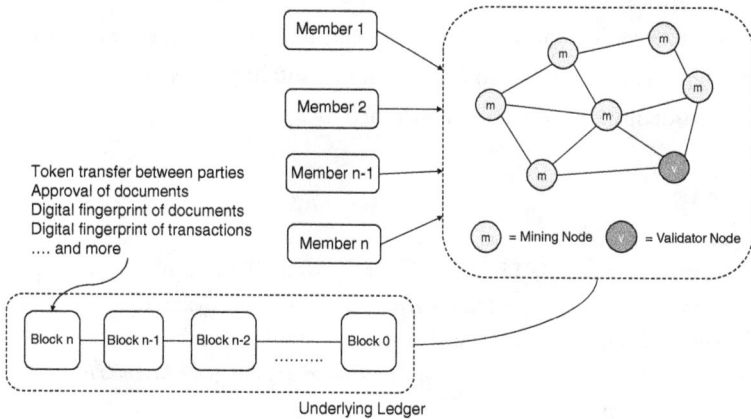

Figure 5.3 Membership-based consortium blockchain with equal access to the members

Nodes verify transactions/blocks as per the consortium rules. In order to add data to the blockchain, a node sends a transaction request to the network of nodes in the consortium. Block validators, or miners, which are special nodes in the consortium network, validate transactions and add them to a block. Hence, validator nodes are known to the network and must be trusted by the consortium. Consortium blockchain is thus a hybrid between private and public blockchains.

Consortium blockchain deployed with a private blockchain utilizing participating peers as nodes and validators poses problems of tampering and 51 percent attacks.[3] It does contain an upside of higher transaction speeds and higher confidentiality because the node network is small, which means transaction confirmation is much faster than public/open blockchain. Consortium blockchains, in a limited sense, can be called semi- or partially decentralized because no single entity has the power to tamper with the blocks and transactions, assuming it is set up that way along with governance rules.

The probability of consortium members colluding to reverse and modify transactions is also real. One way to prove that the data has not been tampered with and preservation of auditability is to periodically publish the hash of a block onto a public blockchain. By doing so, one can be assured that blocks in the interval of two published hashes have not been modified.[4]

The most challenging aspect of forming a consortium blockchain is deploying a sustainable governance structure that oversees the system with regard to keeping the system adequately funded. Doing so may require creating a separate entity to operate and maintain the system on behalf of the consortium, which is then governed by a board.[5]

---

[3]V. Buterin. August 6, 2015. "On Public and Private Blockchains," *Ethereum Blog*. https://blog.ethereum.org/2015/08/07/on-public-and-private-blockchains/.

[4]O. Dib, K. Brousmiche, A. Durand, and E. Thea. 2018. "Consortium Blockchains: Overview, Applications and Challenges," *International Journal on Advances in Telecommunications* 11, no. 1 & 2.

[5]R. Wilson. March 3, 2019. "The Right Way to Do Blockchain Consortiums," *Coindesk*. https://www.coindesk.com/the-right-way-to-do-blockchain-consortiums.

CHAPTER 6

Deconstructing Smart Contracts

Recently I read an interview of an executive who claimed that "smart contracts" have been in existence for over 20 years. This executive's company had just added a smart contract feature in an enterprise system they license to the supply chain industry. As I read the rest of the interview, I quickly realized that the executive was defining smart contract as any form of contract in electronic form, which obviously existed long before 2014. Word plays like this are becoming more common, and truly nonsensical, among executives who are desperate to enter into the blockchain game, trying hard not to distinguish between smart contracts and other forms of electronic contracts.

Smart contracts are not limited to a form of electronic contract. Each smart contract can execute and enforce the contract itself with or without the need for external assistance. It has an executable code that resides on blockchain that interacts with the underlying ledger. Traditional contracts in any electronic form, such as portable document format (PDF) and electronic data interchange (EDI), do not have any such properties. In many ways, smart contracts are more than just contracts; they are a combination of executable code, contract terms, and self-enforcers of the contract.

Self-Execution of Smart Contracts

Once a smart contract is deployed on a blockchain, the contract becomes executable in the sense that the deployer of the contract cannot modify the logic. Figure 6.1 shows the contract code added to the public blockchain. This makes the code not only executable but also immutable. If the

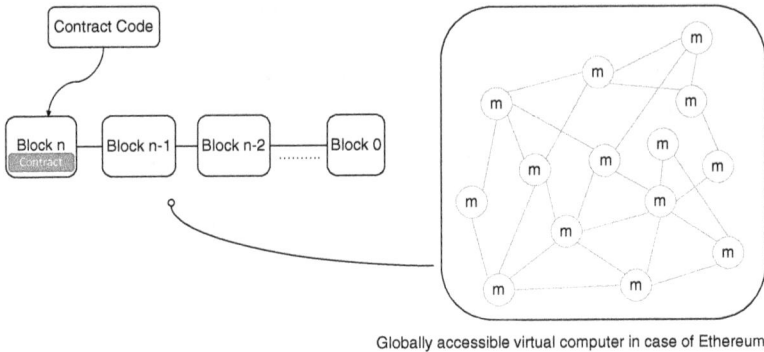

Globally accessible virtual computer in case of Ethereum

Figure 6.1 Contract codes are added to the blockchain along with transactions

contract receives parameters and adequate gas fees from other contracts or individuals, the contract executes the logic it was programmed with in the absence of the original "owner" of the contract. On the Ethereum blockchain, gas fee refers to the expense paid by the users to the miners to perform a transaction on the network.

In the case of Ethereum, smart contracts are executed by the globally accessible virtual machine, comprised of nodes that are also called Ethereum virtual machine (EVM). Adding a smart contract to the Ethereum network means adding a block that is distributed to the network allowing any node to execute the contract as defined by the code. This makes the contract code globally accessible and executable. Executing a smart contract in the EVM requires a gas fee.

Contracts will not execute of their own free will. Hence, smart contracts are somewhat close to autonomous agents living inside a blockchain. The smart contract can continue to "live and breathe" in the blockchain until the owner kills it.

Depending on how the contract is programmed into the blockchain, individuals or machines can interact with the contract to send funds, receive funds, and so forth. Smart contracts are reactive and require external users, or an owner, to execute them using gas fees. However, there are projects, such as Ethereum alarm clock (EAC), whose protocol can be used to trigger smart contracts at a scheduled time. EAC is a service that allows scheduling transactions to be executed at a specific moment in the Ethereum blockchain. Doing so is accomplished by specifying all the details of the transaction desired to be sent, providing up-front gas fees, and allowing the contract to be executed later by an off-chain execution agent called Time Node, acting as the counterparty to transactions.[1]

Create, Use, and Kill

Smart contracts are created by users with a single private/public key. A multisignature or multisig contract is also possible, especially for institutions that require multiple individuals to confirm transactions. Once the smart contract is deployed in blockchain, anybody with access to the public address of the smart contract can interact with it. A public address makes it globally accessible right after deployment. A front end is recommended for smart contract interaction and access control.

Updating and modifying a smart contract means the original owner must kill the smart contract and create a new one, herding users to the new contract or changing the address of the old contract to the new one. Only the original owner who initialized the contract can destroy or kill the contract.

When a contract is killed using the kill function, it is not possible to interact with it anymore. To kill a contract, you need to call *selfdestruct (address)*. Providing an address as the parameter lets you transfer the remaining funds stored in the contract to the address. Killing a smart contract does not remove previous transactions from the blockchain. When a kill function is executed, the smart contract checks for the identity of the function caller and prevents it from getting destroyed by anyone. If you send a transaction, or funds to it, then it is lost permanently.

Here is an example of what *selfdestruct* would look like in a Solidity smart contract function:

```
function kill() public onlyOwner { //onlyOwner is custom modifier}
selfdestruct(owner); // `owner` is the owners address}
```

[1]L. Saether. April 17, 2018. "Ethereum Alarm Clock," *GitHub*. https://github.com/ethereum-alarm-clock/ethereum-alarm-clock/wiki/Quick-Start.

What if the original owner wants to stop the smart contract from execution for the time being for various contractual and technical reasons? Although the function goes against the thesis of unstoppable code and self-execution, the stop/start feature provides many practical benefits. Although the feature is not built into the core code, OpenLaw has built a tool to stop/start a contract from execution by owners who signed the contract. OpenLaw believes such a tool would be useful in executing employment contracts, supply chain workflow, and more in order to comply with existing contractual laws.[2]

Interacting with Smart Contracts

Once a smart contract is deployed in a blockchain, an obvious question is, how does one interact with it? How can someone send funds, input data, receive funds, output data, and so forth? Both Ethereum and EOS smart contracts are accessible via the application programming interface (API). The web3.js library is the official Ethereum JavaScript API. It is a collection of modules that contain specific functionality for the Ethereum ecosystem. The next step is to create a user interface/web application using the hypertext markup language (HTML) and JavaScript for users to interact with the smart contract.

It is also worthwhile to mention that one smart contract calls a function of another already deployed smart contract by referring to its public address. One of the use cases is that the calling smart contract can use the deployed contract as a library. Another use case is to separate logic and data from each other. While the logic contract can be deprecated because of flaws or upgrades, the new contract will simply point to the data contract.

Multisignature Smart Contracts

Smart contracts we've been talking about so far are deployed and owned by a single private key, or single owner. However, if the person who

---

[2]OpenLaw. August 8, 2018. "Controlling Autonomy: A New Tool to Stop Smart Contracts Once Executed," *Medium Corporation.* https://media.consensys.net/controlling-autonomy-a-new-tool-to-stop-smart-contracts-once-executed-bc9de699bca0.

deployed the contract disappears after moving the crypto balance from the contract to his or her wallet, it creates problems of crypto theft.

Imagine a company holding millions of dollars' worth of crypto in a smart contract deployed by the CEO and him or her conveniently disappearing after moving the funds to a personal wallet. To avoid this type of scenario, multisignature or multisig smart contracts are becoming common.

Multisig contracts allow multiple keys, or individuals and entities, to be owners of the contract instead of having only one owner.[3] That means a minimum number and quorum, such as two out of three or three out of five, of keys are necessary when executing owner-based functions in the smart contract. Such functions include balance transfer to other addresses and killing the contract.

Multisig is like requiring multiple people, instead of a single person, in a company to sign a check or execute a legal contract. In a 2/3 contract, if one key is stolen or lost, the other two keyholders can manage the contract to send funds to another address by mutually signing a transaction.

One of the use cases of multisig contracts is to create a third-party arbitrator/mediator and escrow in a two-party transaction. OpenBazaar, a decentralized marketplace to buy and sell goods, uses a similar structure in which a third party approves the payment from buyer to seller. If both buyer and seller agree with the transaction, then the arbitrator is not needed. The smart contract in this case works like a trusted third-party escrow where the funds are held until two-thirds of signatories approve the release of funds from the smart contract.

Regardless of whether they are single signature or multisig contracts, there are more use cases being explored and put into production that emulate activities traditionally done using extensively written paper contracts. The initial coin offering (ICO) craze of 2017 and 2018 is an instance of billions of dollars being raised to fund projects by issuing tokens that were subsequently traded in crypto exchanges. ICOs resemble initial public offerings of companies but without the need for underwriters

[3]C. Lundkvist. August 11, 2017. "Exploring Simpler Ethereum Multisig Contracts," *Medium Corporation.* https://medium.com/@ChrisLundkvist/exploring-simpler-ethereum-multisig-contracts-b71020c19037.

or brokers/dealers. Next came the decentralized autonomous organizations and on-chain governance using smart contracts, explained in later chapters.

Handling Service Exceptions

Smart contracts, as with any other computer program, are optimal in dealing with normal and binary conditions. In transactional systems, such as buying and selling services and goods, most transactions are processed without a hitch.

Take, for example, a truck driver who, after driving 1,000 miles, delivers a shipment to a wrong address given to him or her by the employer. The employer received the address from a broker, who received it from a shipper. The truck driver can execute a claim, after which the system can send the correct address to the driver. The driver or the carrier, not being at fault, may ask for additional fees from the broker or shipper.

If the foregoing scenario occurs, ideally, a new smart contract designed to handle this case can be triggered. All parties agree to additional fees as well as issued payment to the carrier. In the worst-case scenario, both parties may not agree on fees, and the shipment may be left stranded for days until the issue is mediated by a third party.

Dozens of exceptions from the normal operation occur during the normal course of operation that I do not think smart contracts are ready to handle. As shown in Figure 6.2, we need a decision support system that creates the best course of action and lets the smart contract execute the decision made by the system, assuming all the parties have agreed to the decision.

In the case of dexFreight, the internal decision support system needs to trust telematics devices, in-vehicle sensors, and so forth, to send parameters about the real world into smart contracts. Or the system needs context-sensitive artificial intelligence (AI) to operate between oracles and smart contracts to predict the probabilities and consequences of those exceptions and then let smart contracts execute preferred decisions.

The reliance on oracles, external sensors, and telematics devices can be seen both as a strength and as a weakness to increase the adoption of smart contracts in the industrial realm. Oracle is a new concept, and

```
Instrument      ┌──────────────┐
readings        │   Sensors    │
                └──────┬───────┘
                       │
                 Identifies exceptions
                       │
                       ▼
        ┌──────────────┐        ┌──────────────────┐
        │  DSS with AI │        │      Human        │
        │  Determines  │───────▶│ Intervention/Dispute│
        │ Proper Action│        │    Resolution     │
        └──────┬───────┘        └────────┬─────────┘
               ┊                          │
               ┊              Both parties agree
               ┊              on resolution action
               ▼                          │
        ┌──────────────┐                  │
        │    Smart     │◀─────────────────┘
        │  Contracts   │
        └──────┬───────┘
               │
          Take action
               │
               ▼
        ┌──────────────┐
        │   Trigger    │   Note: DSS = Decision Support System
        │   Payments   │
        └──────────────┘
```

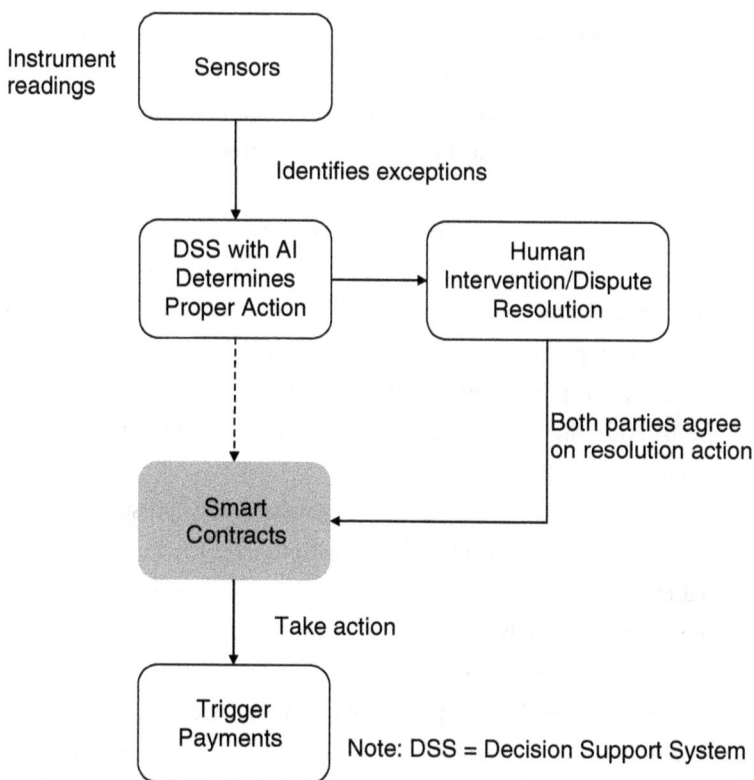

Figure 6.2 *Service exceptions must be performed outside of smart contracts*

external sensors increase the points of entry to attack smart contracts and can be a source of garbage inputs. Hence, AI as a middle layer, in addition to a decision layer, can function as a security layer between oracles or sensors and smart contracts.

"Code Is Law"

We've learned that smart contracts execute themselves as an autonomous agent according to the encoded logic on blockchain without requiring the intervention of the contract's owner. Once the contract is deployed, even the contract's owner cannot change the code's execution logic. The smart contract itself is an enforcer of the logic.

If smart contracts were to become ubiquitous in executing a large variety of contracts other than simply swapping tokens, then this piece of code residing in blockchain could take on a powerful form. There is no stopping us from using the smart contracts to release dividends to equity holders, paying employees, paying counterparties, and more. Until now, these executions were done by humans predicated on traditional legal documents and not by a piece of code.

The phrase "code is law" was coined by Lawrence Lessig in 1999 in his book *Code and Other Laws of Cyberspace*.[4] The phrase defined, in a broader context, how we as consumers of the Internet are regulated by code written by platforms and services that we use over the Internet. In that context, the phrase applies to potentials of smart contracts being a piece of code that can regulate and even enforce our activities on a blockchain.

As Filippi and Hassan noted, smart contracts may "[a]ssume an even stronger role in regulating people's interactions over the Internet as contractual transactions get transposed into smart contract code." They also mention that there will be a "[s]hift from the traditional notion of 'code is law' to the new conception of 'law is code,' or law being defined in code. Our reliance on blockchain technology, via smart contracts, becomes ubiquitous, a notion Filipi and Hassan described as '[t]emptation by the profession to draft legal or contractual rules closer to technical rules.'"[5]

Ubiquity of smart contracts is already prevalent in the tokenization space. I admit that it is yet to take over the traditional commerce industry. Disclaimer: dexFreight is one of those projects attempting to make smart contracts a central, contractual mechanism that allows parties to agree on terms and execute those terms simplest, one of which is issuing payment.

Contracts and Hold-Up Problem

Holden and Malani wrote extensively about hold-up problems in contracts and how smart contracts can be a solution to the problem.[6] A

[4]L. Lessig. 1999. *Code and Other Laws of Cyberspace* (New York, NY: Basic Books).
[5]P. De Filippi and S. Hassan. December 5, 2016. "Blockchain Technology as a Regulatory Technology – From Code is Law to Law is Code," *First Monday*. https://firstmonday.org/ojs/index.php/fm/article/view/7113/5657#author.
[6]R. Holden and A. Malani. May 2019. "Can Blockchain Solve the Hold-Up Problem in Contracts?", *National Bureau of Economic Research*.

simple example of the hold-up problem is as follows. A trucking company agrees with a shipper on a rate of $2.00 per mile to transport a shipment from A to B. Halfway through, the trucking company informs the shipper that unless the rate is increased to $2.50 per mile, it would not deliver the shipment and abandon it in the middle of nowhere. Now, the trucking company can argue in court that circumstances that led to the original rate have changed, and the shipper can argue that the rate was predetermined and agreed on by the trucking company and that the latter should bear the responsibility.

It seems that courts can go either way in terms of deciding the case and allow or disallow the modification sought by a party because it is difficult for the courts to decide whether the change of circumstances presented by the trucking company (in the foregoing case) is valid.

Hence, avoiding hold-ups requires writing a near perfect contract, which is close to impossible, as well known. Holden and Malani argued in their article that smart contracts can be a solution to avoid hold-ups because of its self-execution attribute. One party cannot stop the execution of the smart contract at its own will. There's no room for renegotiation after both parties have signed a smart contract and executed.[7] The solution to any potential problems should already have been encoded in the contract, and any renegotiation can happen only after the contract has executed.

Contracts are complex instruments in which there is always asymmetry of power to one party or the other. Contract negotiations take a long time because both sides want to either tilt the scale toward them or find a balance such that there is symmetry of power. Because smart contracts are definitive, and execution is predefined, such asymmetry can be reduced.

However, currency or assets being transferred by the contract must be digital. Otherwise, the smart contract cannot enforce the agreement between the parties.

[7] O. Meier and A. Sannajust. May 5, 2020. "The Smart Contract Revolution: A Solution for the Hold-up Problem?", *Small Business Economics*. doi:10.1007/s11187-020-00339-7.

Absence of Legal Jurisprudence

Smart contracts are codified agreements between parties in public blockchain. Terms and conditions of the contract are programmed in the contract, which executes itself. Potential use of smart contracts in payments, asset transfer, title transfer, and so forth has been discussed previously.

One of the questions often asked is, are smart contracts legally enforceable? Imagine a situation involving transfer of physical assets such as homes or vehicles. What happens if a digital copy of an asset transfer has occurred but one of the parties decides not to honor it for whatever reason. Can the aggrieved party take the other party to court and show to the judge the existence of asset transfer in a smart contract? Most importantly, will the judge recognize the smart contract as a legal contract?

The Chamber of Digital Commerce released a report in September 2018 and argued that smart contracts do possess necessary components as a contract vehicle under U.S. laws but may not be so within other jurisdictions.[8]

Max Ruskin, in *Georgetown Law Technology Review*, identified several legal issues arising from inflexibility of smart contracts. According to Mr. Ruskin, traditional courts allow discretion, or imperfect performance, in a contract. Smart contracts do not allow ambiguity in performance. Courts in the United States do not demand perfect performance for a contract to be recognized and enforced. The common law doctrine of substantial performance permits a contract to be recognized even if the performance does not fully conform with the express terms laid out. Although not impossible, it would be difficult for a smart contract to code imperfect performances by one or both parties of a transaction.

The second issue that arises is if the courts decide to reverse a decision, how will smart contracts behave when they have already executed and added a transaction to an immutable ledger? This is unlike traditional contracts whose performance can be stopped by the parties either voluntarily or by court order.[9]

---

[8]"Smart Contracts: Is the Law Ready?", *Chamber of Digital Commerce*, 2018.

[9]M. Raskin. 2017. "The Law and Legality of Smart Contracts," *Georgetown Law Technology Review* Revision 305.

Nonetheless, Mr. Ruskin does assert that a clear majority of transactions will be processed by smart contracts to achieve value propositions that come with it. I believe that, until the smart contracts have legal workarounds, initial use cases of smart contracts will be limited to low-value transactions. High-value transactions such as buying/selling homes can happen over smart contracts, but there will be traditional contracts attached to those transactions to address exceptions and human-centric causes such as act of God, force majeure, and so forth.

With regard to inherent inflexibility of smart contracts, Jeremy Sklaroff cautioned that "*a full-scale smart contracting revolution would introduce costs far more extreme and intractable than the ones it seeks to solve. Proponents who argue for a complete replacement of semantic contracts underestimate the power of fluid human behavior and judgment in the contracting process. The flexibility of semantic contracts is a feature, not a bug.*[10]"

Mr. Sklaroff also mentioned, "*Smart contracts that fail to offer semantic and enforcement flexibility will be useful in a very limited set of circumstances. Smart contracts are also meant to operate in the 'real world' — one that is regulated by traditional rules of law.*" Smart contracts will gain significant traction in use cases not heavily regulated by the state and federal laws. Such use cases are crypto token swaps, crypto payments at point of sale, and so forth. We're seeing clear evidence of smart contracts being widely used in those cases but significantly less in high-value, non-crypto transactions. Why would I sell/buy a house using only smart contracts? I still need the legal protection offered by traditional contracts.

Wrapping It with a Ricardian Contract

Ricardian contract was invented by Ian Grigg circa 1995. It is a digital contract that is user friendly to lawyers and at the same time machine readable. The original intent of such contracts was to issue bonds over the Internet backed by a legally defensible contract.

---

[10]J. Sklaroff. 2018. "Smart Contracts and the Cost of Inflexibility," *University of Pennsylvania*, Prize Winning Papers 9.

Mr. Grigg described it as follows[11]: "*A Ricardian Contract can be defined as a single document that is (a) a contract offered by an issuer to holders, (b) for a valuable right held by holders, and managed by the issuer, (c) easily readable by people (like a contract on paper), (d) readable by programs (parsable like a database), (e) digitally signed, (f) carries the keys and server information, and (g) allied with a unique and secure identifier. To uniquely identify the contract, any user can calculate a canonical message digest over the clear signed document.*"

To give a naïve explanation, Ricardian contracts convert traditional contracts, turning them into machine readable and parsable contracts. This makes the contracts legally enforceable because they have all the intents and consequences of traditional paper contracts. The contract is accepted by agreeing to the hash of that contract. The hash is then referred to in the payment process, which can be manual. Hence, execution of payment is separate from the contract itself, which is where smart contracts come in. Since smart contracts assume that counterparties have already agreed to execute a code, they can take the form of a payment executor on behalf of the Ricardian contract. As you can tell, Ricardian contracts are complementary to smart contracts because smart contracts can execute, or transfer and receive funds, on conditions that Ricardian contracts cannot.

Mr. Grigg published an article in 2015 that conceptualized the "Intersection between both types of contracts" and described how both types of contracts are complementary to each other in defining and executing an agreement.[12] Some implementations of Ricardian contracts have emerged, including those by OpenBazaar.

EOS is another blockchain platform that uses a Ricardian + Smart contract model, where parties in the contract, including third-party arbitrators, must sign. In the EOS model shown in Figure 6.3, smart contracts execute the payment and transfer of tokens, whereas the Ricardian side is used in lieu of a traditional legal contract.[13]

---

[11]I. Grigg. "The Ricardian Contract," *iang.org*, https://iang.org/papers/ricardian_contract.html#ref_1, (accessed September 9, 2018).

[12]I. Grigg. February 2015. "On the Intersection of Ricardian and Smart Contracts", *iang.org*, https://iang.org/papers/intersection_ricardian_smart.html.

[13]"What is a Ricardian Contract?" *Block One*. https://eosio.stackexchange.com/questions/1054/what-is-a-ricardian-contract, (accessed July 18, 2019).

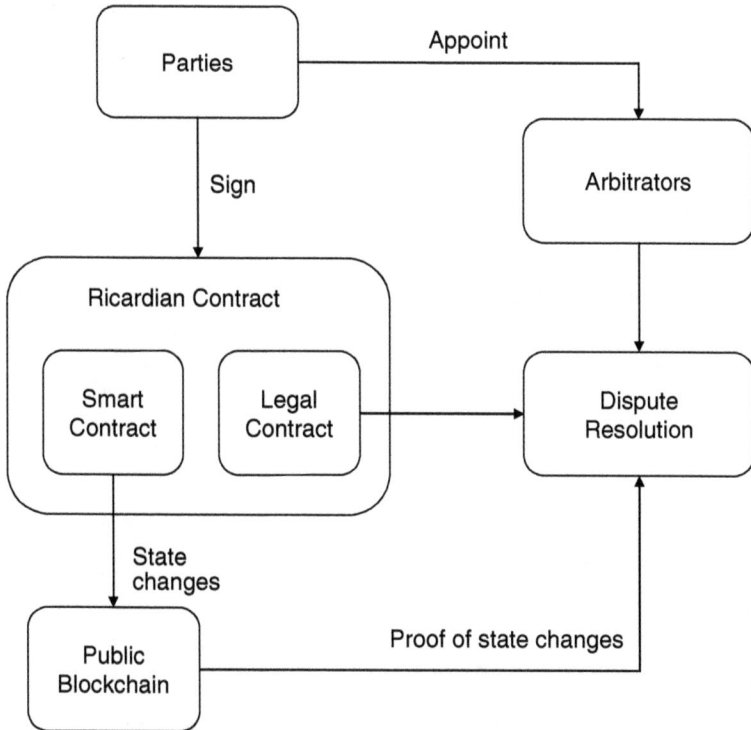

Figure 6.3 **Smart contracts can be supplemented with traditional legal contracts to create complete and executable legal instruments**

The problem with the foregoing model is that the relationship between a smart contract and a legal contract is not clear. Legal contracts may point to a hash of the smart contract as the "executor." What else can be done to keep the relationship dynamic? On the other hand, modifications in legal contracts also need to be tracked, preferably on blockchain.

Another model is adding legal prose into the smart contract itself. However, the idea has been quickly turned down because adding 25 pages of traditional contract language, most of which is never executed, into smart contracts would be a huge waste in gas fees and storage.

From what I've seen, Ricardian contracts are easy to implement. What puzzles me is why its adoption by the industry has been extremely limited given its existence since the nineties. However, discussions about Ricardian contracts are increasingly frequent, especially among the legal professionals desiring to leverage smart contracts as a temporary fix to provide a legal wraparound for smart contracts.

CHAPTER 7

Use of Decentralized Infrastructure for Businesses

By decentralized infrastructure, I mean public blockchain infrastructure such as Ethereum and Bitcoin. Some services are built on top of this infrastructure. I describe how to utilize those services in a later part of the book. In this chapter, I shall talk about what decentralization is in the context of public blockchain as an infrastructure, decentralized protocols, and applications.

Decentralization is all the rage in the blockchain world these days. I must confess that I find it confusing and sometimes even disorienting when describing what decentralization is. Mr. Buterin wrote an interesting blog article in Medium about decentralization and proclaimed that "[i]t is also one of the words that is perhaps defined the most poorly."[1] To paraphrase what Mr. Buterin wrote in the blog, there are three types of decentralized systems—architectural, political, and logical.

Architectural decentralization is all about how computers in the system are arranged. Political decentralization is about control of power over the network—about the number of individuals or organizations that ultimately control the system and computers that are part of the system. Logical decentralization has more of a swarmlike feature.

---

[1] V. Buterin. February 6, 2017. "The Meaning of Decentralization," Medium Corporation. https://medium.com/@VitalikButerin/the-meaning-of-decentralization-a0c92b76a274.

What Does Decentralized Infrastructure Mean?

According to Mr. Buterin, blockchain is architecturally and politically decentralized but logically centralized because there is one agreed upon state. By that definition, Ethereum and Bitcoin both fall into that category. It seems to me, from Mr. Buterin's definition, that a system to achieve all three types of decentralization is quite difficult, perhaps even impossible. He does mention that interplanetary file systems may fall into a logically decentralized system, but is it politically decentralized?

In this chapter, I'll discuss what decentralization means for businesses, whether it's even feasible in a B2B environment, and how it might force businesses to rethink their strategies. I'll also discuss why it is a difficult topic in terms of implementation and my own struggle to define it at dexFreight. I shall also discuss pushbacks and argue that we will see very limited, fully decentralized B2B systems in the foreseeable future.

Unlike other chapters, this one is filled with more questions than answers because that's how we currently stand on these topics.

I submit that both Bitcoin and Ethereum are perhaps the most decentralized infrastructures out there. Bitcoin core developers do have a lot of say in the future path of development, but so do miners and nodes. Major updates to the core protocol must be agreed on by the core developers and powerful miners. Ethereum has the Ethereum Foundation in addition to core developers and miners. The foundation holds a large cache of Ether. Whether the foundation has a lot of influence in future implementation of Ethereum is debatable. Other cryptocurrencies have even more influential companies and core developers behind them.

Balaji Srinivasan, a former chief technology officer of Coinbase, used the Gini coefficient as a crude measure of decentralization of systems.[2] Intuitively, the more uniform the distribution of resources, the closer the Gini coefficient (G) is to zero. In a highly centralized system, G is close to 1. Conversely, in a highly decentralized system $G=0$. Hence, a low Gini coefficient means a high degree of decentralization.

---

[2] B. Srinivasan and L. Lee. July 27, 2017. "Quantifying Decentralization," Medium Corporation. https://news.earn.com/quantifying-decentralization-e39db233c28e.

Censorship Resistance of Decentralized Infrastructure

One of the core value propositions of public blockchain is censorship resistance of the network and the underlying ledger. Censorship resistance, mainly in the blockchain community, means state actors or an institution's ability to shut down the network and/or attack the ledger to double spend transactions. Although double spend attacks don't shut down the network, they will effectively erode the users' confidence in the security of the underlying blockchain. Double spend attacks on confirmed transactions are quite expensive, but on unconfirmed transactions they are feasible. This becomes especially problematic for small transactions that may not be picked up by miners to quickly confirm and get added to the ledger. Mining pools have different policies to confirm unconfirmed transactions.

As the network and the ledger have grown, the financial requirement to shut down the network is becoming larger and improbable. In addition, the computing requirement to double spend transactions or attack the network is also growing exponentially. Obviously, this statement doesn't apply to all blockchain networks, some of which have had to hard fork because of 51 percent attack.

However, censorship resistance can take a different form, in which states may request decentralized platforms to de-platform, or remove access to certain decentralized applications, or dApps, to comply with existing laws and regulations of the country. For example, Tron confirmed that it will be collaborating with the Japanese government to prevent gambling dApps from being accessible within the Pacific island territory.[3] Although dApps run on decentralized networks, de-platforming them from dApp stores can significantly reduce the traction or foot traffic to the application.

Traditional Businesses Using Decentralized Infrastructure

It would be naïve to think that every business in the world will start using public blockchain. That's very unlikely owing to the regulatory and

---

[3]K. Sedgwick. April 4, 2019. "Decentralized Networks Aren't as Censorship Resistant as You Think," Bitcoin.com. https://news.bitcoin.com/decentralized-networks-arent-as-censorship-resistant-as-you-think/.

technical issues that we will discuss throughout this book. However, it is not far-fetched to think that traditional businesses can use decentralized infrastructure to support parts, or the entirety, of their business operation by connecting directly to a public blockchain infrastructure and/or using dApps developed internally or by a third party, as shown in Figure 7.1. This is discussed extensively later on in the book, with only a brief flavor of what that means provided here.

In the chapters titled "Transforming Current Business Models" and "Creating Innovative Business Models," I discuss at length how traditional businesses can leverage public blockchain infrastructure. Essentially, that entails two broad methods, as follows:

- Anchoring some or all of the transactions to public blockchain to provide a much higher level of transparency and security as well as censorship resistance.
- Integrating with new types of business and dApps that are directly built on public, permissionless blockchain. Those applications may be oracles, decentralized finance, arbitration, and so forth.

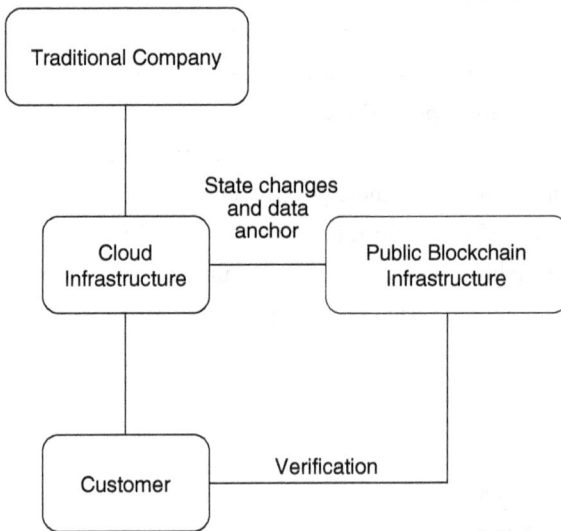

Figure 7.1 *Traditional companies can utilize public blockchain both directly and via API services*

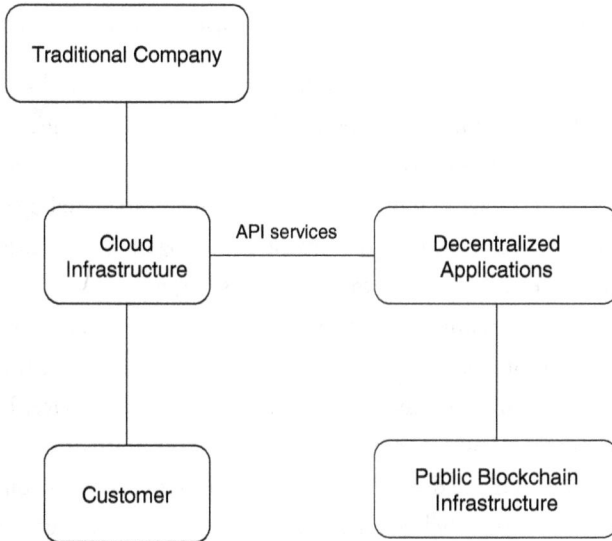

Figure 7.1 (continued)

Decentralized Applications Built on Public Blockchain

Let's take a moment to describe what dApps are.

Decentralized Nature: As their name suggests, dApps store everything on a decentralized blockchain, or any cryptographic technology, to save the app from the perils of centralized authority and place emphasis on autonomous nature.

Incentivization: As the app is based on the decentralized blockchain, the validators of the records on the network must be rewarded, or incentivized, with cryptographic tokens or any form of digital asset that has value.

Algorithm: dApps need to have a consensus mechanism that portrays proof of value in the cryptographic system. Essentially, this endows the cryptographic token with value and creates a consensus protocol that users agree on to generate valuable crypto tokens.

Essentially, dApps are applications that run on decentralized, P2P networks. After the invention of blockchain, dApps have been associated with web applications that use public blockchain to store front- and back-end components, including smart contracts.

Are Politically Decentralized Applications Feasible?

OpenBazaar has shown that B2B applications are technically feasible even though the extent of their political decentralization is questionable because OpenBazaar essentially operates and maintains the marketplace. Assuming OpenBazaar relinquishes control of the protocol to buyers, sellers, and other token holders, they must come together and, through a consensus process, decide how the protocol is upgraded, priced, and governed. Sounds interesting, but why would buyers and sellers want to take control of the protocol and manage it when that's not their core function? Their core function is to buy and sell things in the marketplace. Instead, they will rely on a few active delegates of the community or community representatives to make decisions about the future of the protocol.

Almost all dApps such as marketplace, mobility, insurance, and real estate, are neither politically nor architecturally decentralized. Just because some of them have made their code open source, it doesn't make them decentralized. These applications are still politically, and to a large extent architecturally, controlled and managed by a core group of individuals who are part of a legal entity. This present state might be acceptable for the blockchain community and investors who purchased tokens in public sale. However, over time, these projects will come under intense pressure to decentralize.

I must mention that going fully decentralized with business-to-business applications is infeasible, or at least not yet, for two reasons. First, businesses who sell applications have bottom lines such as revenue and profit and therefore can't operate at a loss for a long period. That requires them to retain control over the system to prevent a competitor from copying their idea and eating up their bottom line.

Second, businesses that buy or subscribe to systems expect a certain level of performance and service from the provider. Businesses don't like to buy free stuff, not for a very long time. Hence, the provider has operating expenses to service their customers, which relates back to the first reason.

CHAPTER 8

Know Blockchain's Limits

One thing public blockchain is good at is maintaining nonrepudiation of transactions in a secure and immutable ledger. This can be a double-edged sword because the ledger cannot guarantee accuracy and precision of attributes in transactions but can guarantee that a transaction was indeed recorded. Hence, the responsibility of adding accurate and precise attributes in transactions added to the blockchain rests outside either by using oracles or through other trusted mechanisms. For example, blockchain by itself cannot verify that a real-estate property being traded has 1.0 acre of land because it must rely on a third party to verify the acreage. However, blockchain can verify that the trade between two parties did occur and was properly recorded. This is one of the biggest limitations of blockchain and probably one of the main reasons for slow adoption of trading nonfinancial or physical assets.

On the other hand, in Bitcoin transactions, the ledger knows, going all the way back to block 0, if an address is attempting to double spend. An address with 1 Bitcoin cannot send 1.01 Bitcoins to another address because the network confirms that the sending address has only 1.0 Bitcoin. Using consensus, such attempts to overspend will quickly get rejected by the network.

At its core, the Bitcoin network doesn't need to call external data sources or oracles to prevent double spending. That's why it is almost a trustless system. However, every time a blockchain network needs to call an external data source to authenticate transaction attributes, concerns about trust appear.[1] Concerns about proper design of the system to authenticate attributes of transactions must be addressed.

---

[1] P. Kravchenko. May 31, 2018. "What Prevents Blockchain from Being Applied to the Real Sector?" *Hackernoon*. https://medium.com/hackernoon/what-prevents-blockchain-from-being-applied-to-the-real-sector-c1d9940bbd7b.

Garbage in Garbage Stays

One of the questions I often get asked is "what happens if someone enters a transaction with wrong data by mistake or on purpose?" In traditional database technology, somebody with appropriate rights can go in and fix the data after the fact. In blockchain, the transaction stays in the network permanently. Isn't that the whole point of immutability? If a node can remove or alter transactions, blockchain would be just another database.

Therefore, extra care is needed before submitting transactions to blockchain. If in a transaction a wrong attribute is attached, then another transaction can be submitted that voids the previous transaction. However, voiding older transactions will be recorded somewhere in the off-chain and sent to all parties involved. Hence, blockchain is a Garbage In Garbage Stays (GIGS) system, in which data, whether garbage or not, stays in the blockchain forever, as shown in Figure 8.1. The effect

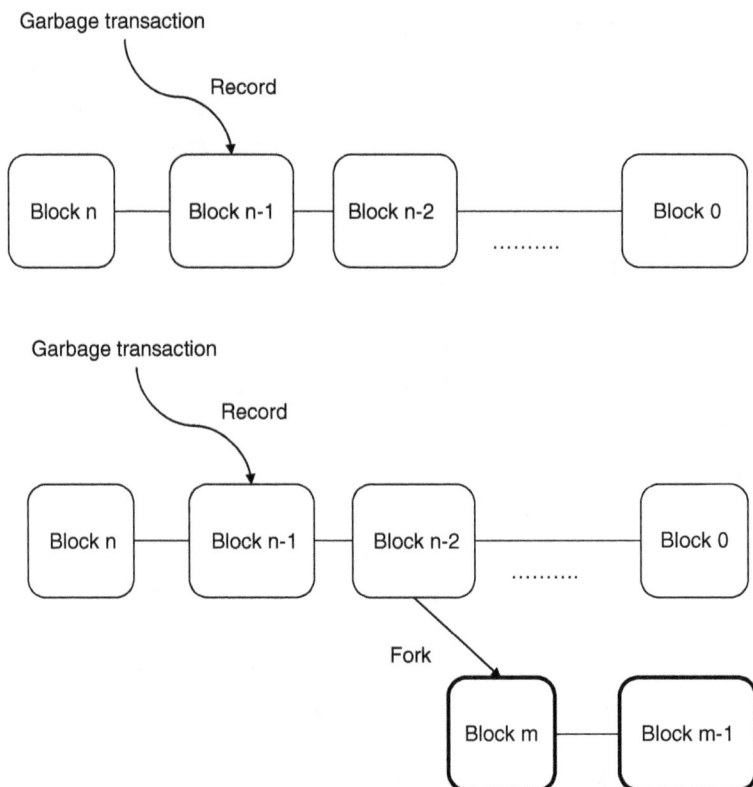

Figure 8.1 Garbage transactions stay in the blockchain forever

of garbage transactions can be nullified by forking the blockchain after the transaction was entered, but doing so every time someone does so is impractical and in the case of public blockchain is unlikely because of mining difficulties.

I strongly recommend that transactions with data attributes such as the amount of crypto, identification of the asset, sensor readings, address, and so forth, be entered from another system rather than by humans to avoid erroneous transactions. This is also a crucial factor in the last mile problem of blockchain. Make the blockchain application as user friendly as possible, and make it less prone to errors before transactions are added to blockchain. If not, data integrity will become the Achilles heel of blockchain.[2]

Last Mile Problem

The last mile is a colloquial phrase widely used in logistics, telecommunications, and cable television to refer to the final leg or segment of the network that delivers data to the end user. In logistics, the last mile is the United States Postal Service (USPS) driver dropping a package at your home. In the case of telecommunication, it is that final segment of fiber optics wire that connects your home to a nearby hub.

An interesting aspect of the last mile problem is that in almost all disciplines, it is the most inefficient and expensive part of the network. In the case of supply chain, it can be up to 30 percent of the transportation cost.[3] That's because last mile delivery typically involves manual processes, capital cost, delivery cost, incorrect addresses, difficulty finding locations, no one at home to receive orders, dogs scaring the delivery guy, and more.

At least you don't have to spend 10 minutes with a delivery person to read and sign a 10-page document or swipe a credit card when USPS

[2]A. Bateman. October 19, 2017. "Blockchain's Garbage In, Garbage Out Challenge," *Supply Chain at MIT*. https://supplychainmit.com/2017/10/19/blockchains-garbage-in-garbage-out-challenge/.
[3]Stigo. October 4, 2017. "The Last Mile – the Term, the Problem, and the Odd Solutions," *Medium Corporation*. https://medium.com/the-stigo-blog/the-last-mile-the-term-the-problem-and-the-odd-solutions-28b6969d5af8.

delivers a package from Amazon. If that were the case, Amazon would be a complete flop.

What does this have to do with blockchain? If you generalize the term last mile, it really means how a blockchain system or application will interface with a physical asset. Or will it still require a trusted intermediary to bridge between the two? Within the cryptocurrency world, last mile is often associated with everyday use and widespread adoption.

Let's take an example of a truck carrying a shipment. Suppose we are building an application to record shipment events in a smart contract and trigger a payment event based on on-time delivery. Carrier A, who was originally contracted to deliver the shipment, gives the shipment to Carrier X without the shipper's consent. Let's assume this is in violation of a contract with the shipper because they want to maintain full visibility of the shipment. How will the blockchain prevent Carrier A from handing over the shipment to Carrier B without using a sensor device alerting the shipper that the shipment has been transferred to Carrier B's truck?

In this example, the application would still rely on Carrier A to be honest and not transfer the shipment to Carrier B or to inform the shipper if it must do so. If not, the smart contract would still have a transaction as Carrier A moves the shipment, with serious legal and financial consequences in case of theft or crash of the shipment.

In the logistics industry, it is called double brokering. Cases such as this may take months, if not years, to settle between the carrier's insurance companies even though the fault lies with Carrier A. Any consolation in this use case is that Carrier A can be flagged postdelivery as having violated the original terms and subsequently penalized. Biometrics and sensor devices may be used to prevent Carrier B from picking the load, but that is still an off-chain solution.

Another example that is gaining media attention is provenance of assets along a complex supply chain using blockchain. Let's assume assets are attached with the radio frequency identification (RFID) transponders and location sensors to enable tracking through the supply chain. It is easy to register unique tags, or sensors, to individual assets, but preventing someone from attaching a wrong sensor to a wrong asset either intentionally or accidentally is difficult. In this case, blockchain will register the wrong transaction. Hence, the system is still prone to human error.[4]

Also worth noting is that in some provenance or asset tracking applications, instead of using unique RFID transponders, smart sensors such as global positioning system (GPS) or humidity sensors may be attached to an asset. At time x, a physical asset is attached to a GPS device. However, at time x+1, the same GPS device may be assigned to another asset and so on. Hence, a second layer of application or even a second blockchain may be necessary to keep track of provenance of GPS devices. However, this still requires correct assignment of GPS devices to unique identification of assets, in which case blockchain cannot prevent the erroneous assignment but can quickly detect the issue after the fact.

In an article, "What Blockchain Can't Do," published in *Harvard Business Review*, authors Tucker and Catalini stated that blockchain cannot help with verifying humanness or the honesty of a buyer's intentions.[5] Verifying who's behind the digital identifier requires offline or off-chain verification. Authors contend that verifying the honesty of users is perhaps beyond any technology we possess today.

Blockchain Is Not a Very Good File Storage

People often mistake blockchain as the next generation of data storage. I do get asked often whether blockchain will replace cloud storage. The correct answer is not straightforward and confuses people even more. Blockchain, in its current form, is best suited to store transactions, which is often a small data packet, aka payload. It essentially stores who sent what to whom—sender's id > asset > receiver's id. So it's natural that people ask whether an asset's image or document associated with it can be stored in blockchain. Yes, the payload can be an image file or PDF file if the

---

[4] A. Anjum, M. Sporny, and A. Sill. 2017. "Blockchain Standards for Compliance and Trust," *IEEE Cloud Computing* 4, no. 4, pp. 84–90.

[5] C. Tucker and C. Catalini. June 28, 2018. "What Blockchain Can't Do?" *Harvard Business Review*. https://hbr.org/2018/06/what-blockchain-cant-do.

underlying protocol allows it. Unfortunately, doing so is expensive, both computationally and financially.

Let's find out how much it costs to store 1 MB of data in Ethereum. To store 1 MB of data in the Ethereum blockchain, users must pay about 625 million GWEI of gas. According to ethgasstation. info, the current average gas price is 3.9 GWEI/gas, which equates to 3.9 × 625,000,000/1,000,000,000 ETH or 2.4375 ETH. At a price of $ 200.00 per ETH, that equals $480.00. On the other hand, sending 1 transaction requires 21,000 GWEI of gas, which translates to $0.01. Also worth noting is that the transaction cost fluctuates with the price of ETH/$.

A frugal way of storing data in blockchain is to store its electronic signature, or hash, and store most of the data somewhere else in distributed storage such as Storj, Filecoin, Swarm, or off-chain in a cloud. By storing the signature along with a time stamp, proof of data ownership can be easily verified.

Blockchain was designed to store transactions, or simple inputs and outputs, not bulky data files. As with any other ledger, it is optimized to store transactions. Who knows, blockchain may evolve to do that in the future. A way around this problem is to store attribute data in an off-chain database and store hash of data in blockchain because hash is much smaller than the attribute data itself.

Vitalik Buterin's Trilemma

Decentralization, scalability, and security are the three key traits of blockchain, as Figure 8.2 shows. Can a blockchain, open or private, achieve all three traits? Mr. Buterin thinks not and says only two out of three traits are achievable.

Decentralization requires consensus between multiple nodes at a transactional level for the network to be censorship resistant. The larger the network, the longer it will take for the network to arrive at majority consensus. Scalability at the network level is a problem because multiple nodes must arrive at a consensus instead of a small handful of nodes. Hence, Layer 2 solutions are being developed using the private channels to communicate transactions where consensus is not required for all transactions. Layer 2 solutions are described later in the book.

Scalability

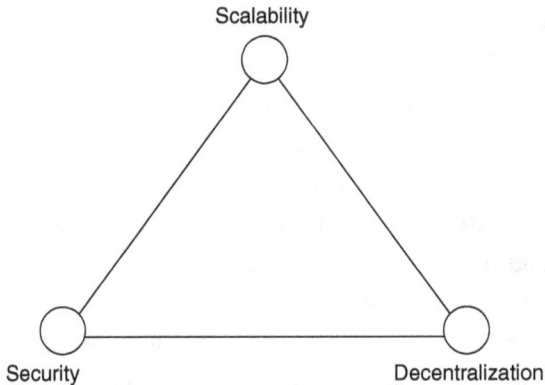

Security   Decentralization

Figure 8.2 Public blockchain's trilemma of scalability, security, and decentralization

Bitcoin, Ethereum, and other decentralized public blockchains have so far demonstrated a high level of security by removing single points of failure. Hence, public blockchains have proven to be highly secure even though transactions per second, or confirmations per second, in the network have gone down. This fact has raised interest in creating Layer 2 solutions. In comparison, private blockchain, with a handful of nodes, can process a much higher number of transactions per second. The downside is that 51 percent attacks on nodes remain easy to accomplish.

Throughput and Latency

Transactions per second, or the measure of throughput, and to some extent latency, is one of the most widely debated topics in blockchain. Transactions per second is a measure of how many transactions the network can confirm in a second. Even after a transaction is added to a winning block, the network confirms transactions only after the block has been synced with the rest of the network. Hence, there is an inversely proportional relationship between the number of mining nodes and transactions per second.

With regard to somebody submitting a transaction to the network, time to confirmation depends not only on the network's capacity to add transactions and sync blocks, but also on the number of other transactions that are in queue since the network doesn't have unlimited bandwidth to process these transactions.

For practitioners like me, you'll be in a constant limbo and in debate with your developers about whether you should use public blockchain networks such as Ethereum or Stellar or create your own network using private platforms such as Hyperledger or Cardano.

There's a big difference between operating a test net within Amazon's servers and operating a main net distributed around the globe.

Speed and throughput come at the expense of decentralization, and the more you increase the former, the more you lose of the latter. Block-chains such as EOS and NEO may be faster than Bitcoin, but they are also highly centralized because they rely on a much lower number of vali-dator nodes, among other things.

CHAPTER 9

Focus on Creating Value

Startups and investors often talk about value creation and value capture. Value creation comes mostly from the product itself as well as the value proposition it provides to users in the form of increased efficiency, increased productivity, and lower cost. Value capture is like harvesting a crop and selling it in the market. Value capture methods include monetization, liquidity, and so forth.[1] Experts will tell you that creating value before capturing it is important because most users have a learning curve to adopting new products before they realize its full potential.

Because blockchain is a nascent technology, creating value is still an ongoing effort, and new value propositions are still emerging. In that regard, most people are still fuzzy about value propositions, how to capture value, monetizing and pricing dApps, and financially sustaining decentralized platforms.

However, blockchain has proven and continues to provide significant value of verification of state changes, ledger, documents, contracts at a much lower cost than traditional methods and without intermediaries. The value created by the low cost of transaction verification made cryptocurrencies possible. Smart contracts later showed that blockchain's value can be extended to contracts that result in nonfungible asset transfers. This ability to verify state (of transactions) at a lower cost has proven to be a valuable function for network participants.[2]

---

[1] The Venture CFO. January 22, 2015. "What is the Difference Between Creating and Capturing Value?", *Venture CFO*. http://theventurecfo.com/blog/2015/01/23/what-is-the-difference-between-creating-and-capturing-value.

[2] C. Catalini and J. Gans. June 2019. "Simple Economics of the Blockchain," *National Bureau of Economic Research Working Paper No. 22952.*

Because the cost of verification is low, participants in those transactions can be incentivized to perform actions that create network effects at a much lower cost than traditional ways of, let's say, marketing, rewards, and stocks. This theory has been put in place in decentralized autonomous organizations (DAOs) and other token-powered platforms, which I discuss later.

Proof of {X}

Anchoring information to the blockchain and using it to prove that the information exists, and hasn't been altered, is all the rage these days. Protocols and infrastructure exist to verify proof of existence, proof of integrity, proof of ownership, and so forth. Whereas the actual document is stored off-chain or in a decentralized storage, hash, or a digital fingerprint of a document, is added to the public blockchain. That sounds like a notary or attestation service on blockchain. There are numerous services such as Tierion, Poex, and Stampery that provide proof of existence services for a nominal fee.

As Figure 9.1 shows, hash of the user data, or document, you wish to time-stamp is created and turned into a Bitcoin address. By making a small payment (a Satoshi, or 0.00000001 Bitcoin) to the address, the payment is stored on the blockchain, Bitcoin in this case, along with the address you paid to. Since only the hash is stored on the Bitcoin blockchain, no one can tell what data you stored, but given the prehashed data, you can prove the data was created prior to the block that contains the payment made to that address.

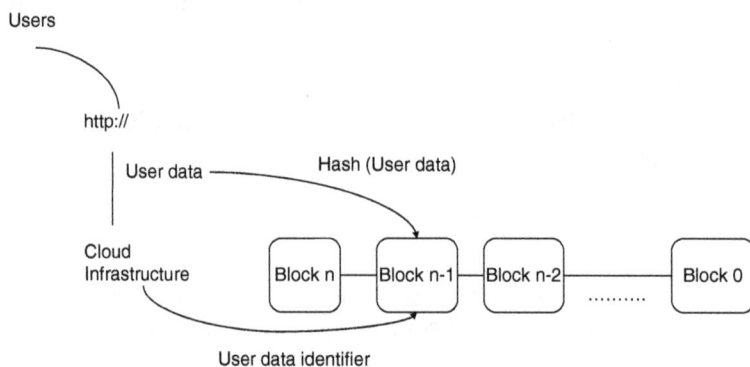

Figure 9.1 Hash of user data added to blockchain as a proof of existence and integrity

Once the transaction is confirmed, the document is permanently certified and proven to exist at least as early as the time the transaction was confirmed. If someone creates a second hash of the same document and adds to the blockchain, the second hash is not the same as the first.[3]

It is important to note that proof of existence does not provide proof of ownership or authenticity.[4] The proof of existence does not provide any information about the source of the information and only communicates that a document, or a piece of data, exists at a specific point in time. The proof of existence of an asset or token must be supported by its proof of ownership. On chain, ownership of the transaction that was used to register the token or asset is signed by a private key.

However, physical assets such as homes, cars, and stocks that are regulated must be tied to legacy identity. Whoever owns the private key must be tied to the legacy identity. This brings up the issue of asset custody and identity registration services provided by a trusted third party.

Proof of ownership and/or proof of existence of a document can be proven by adding a digital hash of the documents such as invoice, waybill, bill of lading, tickets, certificates, and so forth. By comparing the digital hash of a new document with the hash of the original document, one can determine whether the document has been tampered with. To ensure that the original document's hash exists, the hash is recorded with a transaction in the blockchain. Figure 9.2 shows how the hash (or digital fingerprint) of documents is compared in the blockchain. This also ensures that the original document has not been tampered with. Such a method of verifying the proof of integrity ensures that the asset, or attributes, has not been tampered with.

Proof of {X}, as I call it, is critical in creating a new tokenized economy. If we were to convert assets to nonfungible digital tokens, then all three proofs of existence, ownership, and integrity must be implemented. This implementation ensures that tokens representing assets can be properly

---

[3]"Proof of Existence", *NewsBTC*, https://www.newsbtc.com/proof-of-existence/, (accessed September 23, 2018).

[4]M. Greco. April 10, 2018. "Does Proof of Existence establish Provenance?", *Medium Corporation*. https://blog.chronicled.com/does-proof-of-existence-establish-provenance-5028fbd8c6da.

Authentic Document

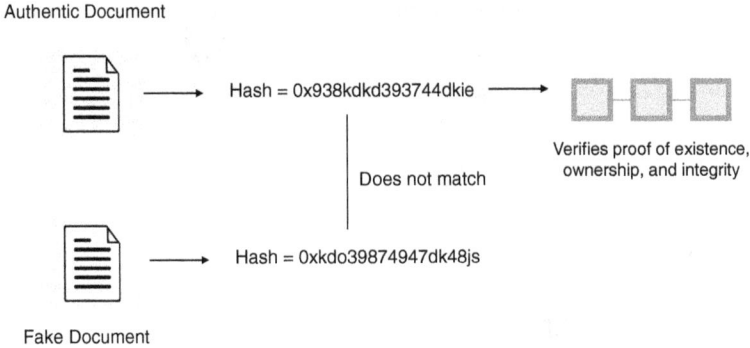

Hash = 0x938kdkd393744dkie ——→

Verifies proof of existence,
ownership, and integrity

Does not match

Hash = 0xkdo39874947dk48js

Fake Document

Figure 9.2 Comparison of authentic and fake documents by comparing hashes recorded in blockchain

transferred, shared, and distributed with a minimized role of intermediaries who would traditionally perform these three functions, replaced by properly designed smart contracts.

Provenance of Decisions

In multistakeholder systems such as airports, maritime ports, health insurance markets, and international supply chains, managing provenance of decisions is critical to aligning incentives of the stakeholders. By decisions I mean approvals along a chain of command, along with verifications and validations of a decision or a physical document. IBM noted in its blog that a typical shipment can pass through as many as 30 unique organizations and generate 200 different communications on its passage.[5] By "typical," it probably meant international shipments from end to end. Domestic shipments do not have to pass through 30 unique organizations, but only a handful. A port in Mexico, where I led a blockchain proof of concept project, has over six agencies, public and private, touch the same document describing shipment information before loading onto a waiting ship. The shipment will go through a similar rigorous process at its destination port before it is released.

---

[5]T. Scott. April 20, 2018. "Enterprise-Ready Blockchain Brings Transparency to Supply Chains," *IBM Corporation*. https://www.ibm.com/blogs/blockchain/2018/04/enterprise-ready-blockchain-brings-transparency-to-supply-chains/.

Ports in many countries are coping with increased volume in and out of limited footprint ports. Hence, the ports must process the containers much faster without compromising the underlying process of information validation and verification. Blockchain will greatly assist because it reduces the need for visual verification of documents moving through a single window system, thereby increasing the throughput of containers in and out of the port.

At ports, agencies must operate with trust, and therefore transparency and accountability are critical. Hence, immutable provenance of decisions pertaining to information verification keeps track of who approved what and when, who sold assets when and to whom, and who approved what and when.

Ports are a great example of where shipping manifests are verified and approved by multiple entities such as a customs agency, terminal operators, port authority, or banks before a ship is loaded. In such a multiparty environment, it is important to track provenance of decisions in the workflow in order to create an accountable and transparent environment. Figure 9.3 shows manifests-related documents produced by various stakeholders in the container export process are recorded in the blockchain using smart contracts. This ensures that the documents are not forged, and the stakeholders can ensure that no unauthorized containers enter the port or are loaded onto a ship.

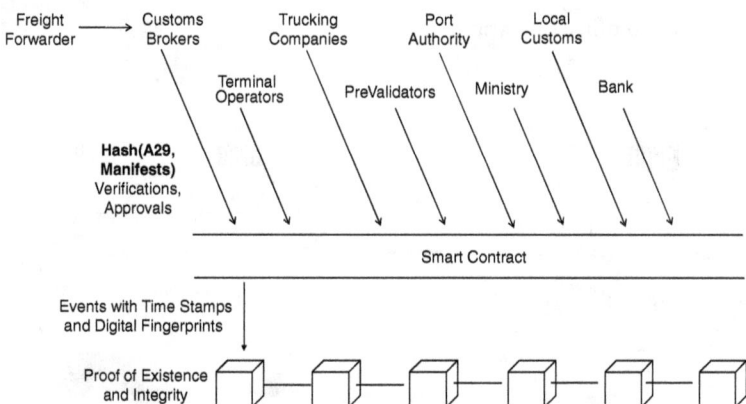

Figure 9.3 Hashes of shipping manifests during the container export process added to blockchain

In the ports project, accountability was designed around prove-nance of decisions by public and private entities. Such decisions were time-stamped and recorded in an immutable ledger that no single entity can unilaterally modify to allow containers to enter the port. This ensures that public entities are not providing favors to any company.

Chain of Custody of Assets

One of the benefits of smart contracts is that every transaction is signed with the public keys of parties involved and stored in an append-only immutable database. Traceability and provenance of decisions on blockchain are simple to implement because parties agree that no single party can unilaterally tamper with transactions. Asset transfers are a typical occurrence in supply, securitization, and so forth. Title companies and other intermediaries play the role of a neutral third party to guarantee that asset transfers will take place and have taken place between transacting parties. This is also typical in food and pharmaceuticals traceability, which requires transacting parties to notify each other of transfer of ownership of goods during supply chain.

In Figure 9.4, n_x are the transacting parties. It shows an example of container shipments changing owners several times before they reach a consignee while the container is on the way to the consignee. The current process of maintaining a paper trail is costly for all transacting parties. If all parties agree that instead of extensive documentation, they use public blockchain to maintain a trail of transfer decisions, then it will reduce costs back to office operation.

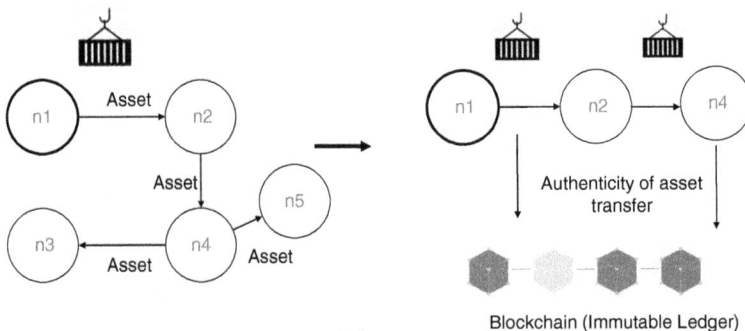

Figure 9.4 Ownership change of assets is recorded in an immutable ledger

By doing so, the cost of sending and settling final invoices will also be simplified. For external and internal auditors, tracing ownership and sender's and receiver's public key addresses is simple and indisputable because those transfers are encoded within blockchain transactions.

Payments and Settlements

One of the biggest challenges with businesses is settling invoices and issuing payments. Health care, logistics, and insurance companies have armies of accountants handling back office operations to verify, validate, and approve invoices sent by vendors and contractors. There is no such thing as intelligent filtering of invoices in which X percent of invoices are automatically approved by an algorithm for settlement. By sharing transaction terms and conditions in immutable smart contracts, invoices don't have to be reconciled, which is often the most time-consuming step before issuing payment.

For this to happen, both parties need to maintain, or at least agree on, the common data definition of terms and conditions and resulting invoice. That is the difficult part because there are no common data definitions or businesses to maintain their own nomenclature and practices. In addition, both parties need to agree to honor the smart contracts that define the terms and conditions of payments and also agree on conditions that trigger payments by smart contracts.

Such conditions may include proof of delivery, proof of completion of tasks, proof of receipt of goods, and so forth. If these conditions can be digitally confirmed by both parties, then they can be sent to smart contracts using oracles, described later, and issue payments without even requiring invoices.

A furniture importer in South Florida once told me that she had over a dozen accountants verifying every invoice they receive from suppliers all over the world. Before an accountant issues a payment, he or she must (1) ensure invoices are correct with names, addresses, and so forth of the suppliers, (2) ensure the amount is the same as the one previously agreed on, which means they must cross-check with price quotes from the exporters, and (3) verify that the furniture has been received in the conditions agreed on.

The first two tasks can be automated with artificial intelligence and clever optical character recognition algorithms. The third task requires, at least in this case, visual inspection by someone in the company specially mandated and competent to inspect received furniture and trigger "proof of receipt." Hence, unless all three tasks can be fully digitized, the benefits of using smart contracts are half baked.

Tokenization of Nonfungible Assets

Tokenization is a digital representation of ownership of an asset. It converts ownership of assets into tokens, which can then be recorded and transferred using blockchain. Tokenization allows assets that are difficult to be traded and liquidated to be done so easily using smart contracts, which maintains an immutable ledger of transfers and ownership of tokens. Such a transfer of tokens would be instantaneous and verifiable in the blockchain.

For example, a piece of land worth $100,000,00 can be tokenized as 100,000 tokens. In the absence of tokens, there is no way of owning $1.00 worth of land. By tokenizing the land, someone can hold 1 token worth $1.00 equivalent of land and thereafter easily trade and transfer the token. By extrapolating that idea allows any physical asset to be tokenized and traded to create immediate liquidity of the asset if doing so makes economic and legal sense.

Fungible assets, such as company stocks, precious metals, and natural resources, are traded daily without tokens. However, these trades are expensive because they require the involvement of trusted intermediaries to facilitate asset transfers and maintain ledgers. They are also a lot easier to tokenize because they can be divided into smaller pieces. A barrel of crude oil can be divided into several gallons without changing its inherent market value.

Pricing the value of fungible assets is easy because they are already traded in the market and possess a reference price. We know the price of a barrel of crude oil because they are traded on the Chicago Mercantile Exchange. The sale, or transfer, of tokens would be recorded on the blockchain, and traders have the option to divide the tokens into smaller pieces.

Nonfungible assets such as copyrights, art pieces, domain names, and patents are difficult to price. We do not hear about patents being traded daily on an online exchange. Nonetheless, they are still assets and are easy to tokenize if prices are defined, and this is a challenge by itself. Tokenizing a work of art means creating its digital signature, which cannot be altered.[6] As Figure 9.5 shows, a certified curator verifies that there is an art piece and that it belongs to someone specific. A digital signature of the art piece is created and stored in a blockchain. This ensures that you are not creating digital signatures of an art piece in a museum. Tokens representing monetary value and ownership of the art piece are issued using a smart contract.

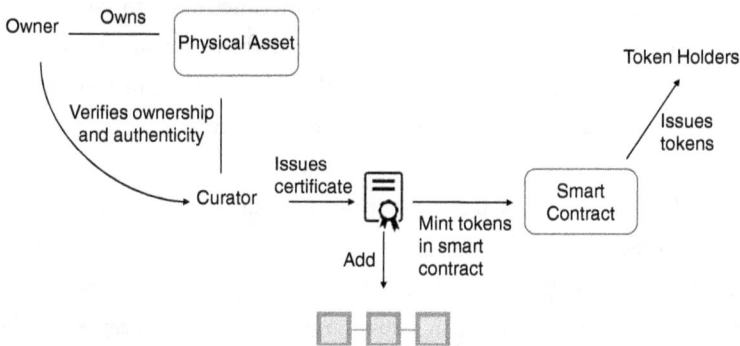

Figure 9.5 Issue ownership tokens representing a digital asset using smart contracts

The digital token representing a unique piece of art can then be further divided into smaller tokens. In doing so, shares, so to speak, of a unique piece of art can be traded, and ownership can be distributed. The difference between ERC-20 fungible tokens and ERC-721 standards for nonfungible tokens is the need to keep track of ownership of smaller tokens when they are first awarded and later transferred.

The concept of a nonfungible token applies to fractional ownership of assets, such as cars, boats, homes, and trucks. More than one person will own a car based on agreement on who will use it and when it was encoded in a smart contract. This will reduce the cost of car ownership because risk is distributed among more than one person.

---

[6]O. Dale. July 31, 2018. "What is Tokenization? Democratizing Ownership and Real-World Assets on the Blockchain," *Blockonomi*. https://blockonomi.com/tokenization-blockchain/.

One of the nonfungible assets that I am excited about is invoices. Especially in supply chain and manufacturing, it takes days and weeks for a service provider to get paid after submitting an invoice to the purchaser of a service. Invoice financing, as it is known in the industry, involves the service provider with an invoice seeking financing from a financial institution such as a bank.

The financial institution, or lender, will charge the service provider 3 to 5 percent, as is the case in the United States, after careful vetting of the invoice. The vetting process involves validating the invoice from the service purchaser. It may require hours, sometimes days, to contact the purchaser. If the invoice had been generated from the smart contract, which is signed by the service purchaser, then the financial institution can simply validate the invoice by auditing the smart contract.

The invoice can be validated in seconds rather than days and with little effort. Also, the financial institution doesn't have to charge a 3 to 5 percent fee because the cost of back office operation would reduce significantly. Assuming tokenized lending will greatly reduce the operational cost of invoice lending, will it allow large institutions to serve smaller businesses using blockchain as a trusted ledger? If that happens, then smaller lenders will compete in that space with bigger institutions. How would that impact the lending industry? If an invoice is tokenized, then it can also be broken into pieces, which means multiple lenders can finance a single invoice and spread their risk. Tokenization further increases the velocity of asset trading if it supports faster clearance of payments.

Since tokens are stored in a smart contract, holders of tokens can sell them to anyone in the world at any time and get paid in another token or cryptocurrency without waiting for bank transfers.[7] However, handling of the underlying assets must be done with transparency and security. He also makes an interesting argument that the new asset class will have to satisfy the highest custodian standards and be subject to periodic audits.

---

[7]D. Raykhman. April 19, 2018. "Asset Tokenization, What, Why, and How," *Medium Corporation*.https://medium.com/coinmonks/asset-tokenization-what-why-and-how-73650c49afe0.

Less Verification Cost Means Reduced Transaction Cost

As I indicated in the introductory part of this chapter, blockchain has the potential to reduce the verification cost of transactions. In Bitcoin, if you are not going to wait for 51 percent of the nodes to confirm your transaction, then whether you are sending $1.00 million worth of Bitcoin or $1.00 worth of Bitcoin, the protocol treats both verifications the same way—the underlying proof of work mechanism of consensus. The same concept applies to Ethereum and smart contracts. Whether the contract is built to transact $1.00 or $1.00 million, the system verifies and executes both contracts the same way, unless you want to increase the gas fee for faster confirmation.

There is no doubt that transferring cryptocurrencies is inexpensive and cheaper than bank-to-bank transfer because the cost of verifying transactions by the banks is expensive on account of national and international banking laws, KYC regulations, administrative costs, and so forth.

CHAPTER 10

Transforming Current Business Models

Information about quantifiable benefits from implementing blockchain technology is scarce. Although we know of hundreds, if not thousands, of proof of concepts and although pilots all over the world have been implemented, pre- and postquantitative benefits of such projects are difficult to find. There is hardly any information about return on investment, cost-benefit analysis, time savings, performance enhancements, and other indicators that executives can use as a reference.

The absence of quantifiable benefits may be one of the reasons holding the technology back from widespread adoption in the enterprise world.

I've written with some authority in this chapter and the next why and how blockchain will transform existing business models and create new ones. However, these claims and opinions lack evidence to quantify their benefits. I'm hopeful that we will hear more on this topic in the future. For example, Lui and Ngai analyzed the impact on firms' market value based on 133 blockchain projects by 77 firms.[1] They found evidence of long-term positive return of firms' market value. The projects they analyzed involved collaboration of some kind using blockchain technology.

Cross-Jurisdictional Payments

Two of the most common and legal use cases of blockchain in cross-jurisdictional payments are global remittance and settling cross-border payments for trade financing.

---

[1] A. Lui and E. Ngai. 2019. "The Long Term Effect of Blockchain Adoption on Firm Value," *Proceedings of the 25th Americas Conference on Information Systems*, Cancun, Mexico.

Global remittance refers to money being sent by individuals working in one country back home to another part of the world. According to the World Bank, global remittances, which include flows to high-income countries, reached $689 billion in 2018.[2] The World Bank says remittance is the biggest external source of funding for many countries in South Asia, Latin America, and so forth.

The report also mentions that the global average amount paid by individuals in fees to financial institutions and money transmitters was around 7 percent in 2019. However, the cost of transmission is extremely nuanced and depends on many factors such as the origin and destination countries, presence of bans, and the receiving region's economic activities. The World Bank report also noted that regions where banks have a greater presence had a higher cost, which is counterintuitive.

Hence, the obvious question is "Why hasn't the use of cryptocurrencies scaled as a competing form of global remittance?" Why can't a Nepali construction worker in Doha send cryptocurrency to his or her family back in a remote part of Nepal instead of fiat and save money on transmission fees? Cryptocurrencies are meant to be borderless and stateless. They are borderless in that their use is not limited to any country, region, or jurisdiction. All anyone needs is a decent connection to the Internet. They are stateless in that they are not controlled by a government.

I posit that the reason crypto hasn't scaled exponentially within the global remittance scene is the first and last mile problem, especially for customers who do not have access to bank accounts or easy access to the Internet to buy and transfer cryptocurrencies. What regional banks and money transmitters like Western Union do well is to solve the first and last mile problem by creating physical touch points with end users locally through association with stores, local banks, and so forth. With Western Union, you can send money even though you and your recipient do not have bank accounts. With cryptocurrency, for most people, you need to have bank accounts to use exchanges like Coinbase, Binance, or Circle to buy Bitcoin and convert to and from local currency.

---

[2]World Bank. April 08, 2019. "Record High Remittances Sent Globally in 2018," *World Bank*. https://www.worldbank.org/en/news/press-release/2019/04/08/record-high-remittances-sent-globally-in-2018.

BitPesa is an Africa-based startup that has solved the last mile problem by allowing money senders to send funds in Bitcoin, charge a small percentage fee, and pay the recipient in a local currency and vice versa using a local bank. BitPesa is now serving importers and exporters across Africa by facilitating seamless trading and payment exchange services using Bitcoin as an exchange currency instead of the dollar, especially for international trade, which comes with huge bottlenecks and bank involvement, raising the exchange fee and processing time. By using Bitcoin as a currency of exchange, it has been able to provide money transmission services with 3 percent fees, a unique achievement in that continent. However, BitPesa is still dependent on local banks to hold local current and pay recipients on behalf of the sender.

The use of cryptocurrency by traders, importers, and exporters to pay for imports and exports is still rare because of the highly regulated environment, including KYC, that these companies must comply with. This point goes along with the fact that they often rely on a line of credit issued by their local banks before starting the import and export process in which the importer's bank guarantees the availability of payment to the exporter's bank.

An exporter may use the line of credit to obtain a loan from the same or a different bank to produce the good. The line of credit along with a contract between importer and exporter then becomes part of the documentation to obtain insurance, government permits, future payments to customs brokers, freight forwarders, and so forth.

Because the processes of trade finance and the import/export of goods involves diverse stakeholders with dozens of documents that need to be cross-validated, a process that often takes days, the trading community has been experimenting with blockchain technology to create an open ledger that is available only to the consortium.

Deloitte estimates that "business-to-business payments with blockchain result in a 40 to 80 percent reduction in transaction costs and take an average of four to six seconds to finalize compared to two to three days using the standard transfer process."[3] Projects like Marco Polo and We-trade are experimenting with the involvement of consortiums consisting of banks, exporters, and logistics companies. Participation of the

---

[3]Deloitte. 2016. "Cross Border Payments on Blockchain," *Deloitte*. https://www2 .deloitte.com/content/dam/Deloitte/global/Documents/grid/cross-border-payments.pdf.

stakeholders has become the norm to move forward with these types of consortium pilot projects and guarantee future adoption.

Decentralized Arbitration

Once a party or parties decide that the mediation will not or cannot produce a desirable resolution, they may elect to go to arbitration and even to litigation. Like mediation, arbitration is a private process in which disputing parties agree on one or several individuals that can decide about the dispute after receiving evidence and hearing arguments.

Arbitration is different from mediation in that the neutral arbitrator has the authority to decide on the dispute. The arbitration process is like a trial in that the parties make opening statements and present evidence to the arbitrator. After the hearing, the arbitrator issues an award to a party. The arbitration process may be either binding or nonbinding. When arbitration is binding, the decision can be enforced by a court and can be appealed only on very narrow grounds. When arbitration is nonbinding, the arbitrator's award is advisory and can be final only if accepted by the parties involved.

Several arbitration administrators and organizations provide arbitration services. Two such agencies are American Arbitration and the Transportation and Logistics Council, also known as the Transportation Arbitration Board. The board, which is a nonprofit, specializes in arbitration of shipper-carrier agreements.

Arbitration administrators resolve disputes without requiring parties to be physically present, providing much faster and cheaper resolution than offline. In both agencies, arbitrators are drawn from a national roster of experts who are called upon to become arbitrators. Agencies vet these individuals to ensure they are trained, experienced, and conflict free.

Enforcement procedures for arbitration awards are governed primarily by the Federal Arbitration Act (FAA) and the Uniform Arbitration Act (UAA). An arbitration award can be easily filed in a county or state court and be confirmed as a court judgment, which can then be used to collect payment from the losing party. In some cases, the losing party may wish to vacate the award either partly or entirely, or the winning party may wish to seek modification or correction of the award. Both the FAA and UAA provide for these options. However, a party's ability to vacate an award is not open ended. This may not be the case in every country. Local laws govern the enforceability of arbitration awards. However, cross-border disputes can be resolved using the New York Convention.

Numerous decentralized arbitration services and protocols have emerged, such as Open Court and Kleros. Their methodology of arbitrating claims may differ, but most of them clash with existing U.S. arbitration laws. For example, Kleros uses anonymous arbitrators, contrary to U.S. laws, which state that parties in dispute shall be provided with an arbitrator's information to ensure impartiality.

In the case of cross-border arbitration, involving disputing parties in two different countries, these protocols may conflict with the New York Convention. Hence, decentralized arbitration may not be enforceable in your jurisdictions in case you have to take the losing party to a local court if the party vacates the award by the arbitrator.

However, if both parties opt in to a smart contract-based arbitration in which they are part of a multisignature smart contract or a Ricardian contract, then one party can raise a dispute and the third-party arbitrator, or signatory in the contract, can lock up the contract until the dispute has been resolved and payment settled. OpenBazaar uses a similar concept to resolve disputes, as shown in Figure 10.1. It is unclear whether the disputing parties can modify the award once the third party has settled using the smart contract and whether they can enforce the award in a local court for settling more than the amount held in the smart contract.

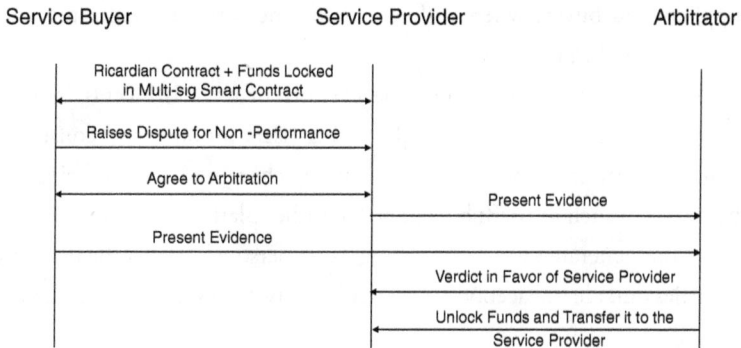

Service Buyer	Service Provider	Arbitrator
Ricardian Contract + Funds Locked in Multi-sig Smart Contract		
Raises Dispute for Non -Performance		
Agree to Arbitration		
	Present Evidence	
Present Evidence		
	Verdict in Favor of Service Provider	
	Unlock Funds and Transfer it to the Service Provider	

Figure 10.1 Third-party arbitrator in the smart contract with ability to release or freeze funds

If smart contracts are to handle disputes, then crypto lawyers should develop methods to:

- Embed dispute resolution function into smart contracts.
- Ensure that a third-party arbitrator can easily request and extract information from smart contracts as evidence.

Nonetheless, smart contract-driven arbitration will greatly enhance the gig economy, in which people from different jurisdictions provide services because there are limited resources or legal recourse to execute a traditional arbitration process. I believe this will reduce the cost and speed of arbitration.

Rise of Token-Powered Platforms

In their book, *Platform Revolution*, Parker et al. defined token-powered platforms as a business that matches external producers with consumers, creating value by enabling participants to exchange goods, services, and social currency.[4] Platforms like this invert the traditional pipeline model to create a value-community of users. The book mentions Facebook, Uber, AirBnb, and others as examples of platforms that foster matches, two sides of supply and demand, to utilize the power of a network of users to create value.

Until the platform model came around, the pipe business model had been the dominant model. Companies create objectives, or services, and sell them downstream to consumers, or buyers. Think of this as a linear flow of supply and demand. In the platform business there are several suppliers and buyers where different items and services are created and consumed within the network.

Within the platform model, the network of users is incentivized by the value of services and things that other users produce and consume. Some platform keepers generate revenue by charging users for being on the platform such as AirBnb or Expedia. Other platforms use a freemium model but generate revenue by selling users' personal data in the network to parties outside it. Facebook sells user identity, behavior, and preferences

---

[4]G. Parker, M. Alstyne, and S. Chaudhry. 2016. *Platform Revolution - How Networked Markets Are Transforming the Economy - and How to Make Them Work for You* (New York: W. W. Norton and Company).

to companies that are not part of the network or outside the network.[5] It has been well recorded that Google's biggest revenue comes from selling ad space.[6] As Andrew Lewis said, "If you're not paying for it, you're not the customer; you are the product."[7]

Traditional platforms have created identity and privacy issues among the network of users. In a crypto-powered platform, governance is pushed to the network, which makes important decisions about the rules and evolution of the platform. Participants in the network also propose improvements and stake their position during voting. Ethereum has been following a similar governance model since its inception in 2014. MakerDAO uses staked voting by its token holders to approve changes in network stability fees.

Figure 10.2 shows how platforms like Ethereum, MakerDAO use tokens to incentivize the stakeholders to create work and increase

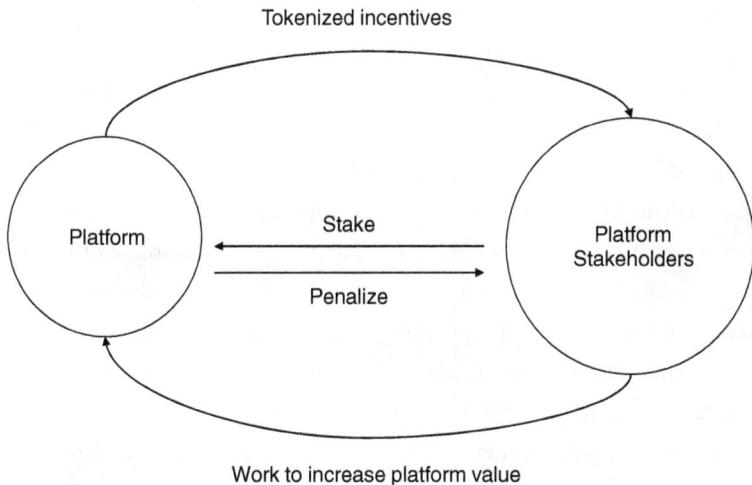

Figure 10.2 Tokens as incentives to work, stake, and penalize stakeholders in platforms and marketplaces

---

[5]B. O'Connell. October 23, 2018. "How Does Facebook Make Money? Six Primary Revenue Streams," *TheStreet Inc.* https://www.thestreet.com/technology/how-does-facebook-make-money-14754098.

[6]G. Fotiadis. February 11, 2018. "How does Google Earn Money? As Simple as That," *Hackernoon.* https://hackernoon.com/how-does-google-earn-money-as-simple-as-that-60c5b399100e.

[7]A. Lewis. September 13, 2010. "If You Are Not Paying for It, You're Not the Customer, You're the Product Being Sold," *Twitter.* https://twitter.com/andlewis/status/24380177712.

the value of the platform while using the tokens to stake for/against governance-related decisions. Tokens have proven to be a valuable mechanism to incentivize stakeholders in modern platforms.

Smart Contract-Powered Data Renting

Companies are in the business of creating, holding, and reselling data. As they say, data is the new oil. Google, Facebook, and Amazon aggregate massive amounts of user data through platform usage. Data aggregators such as Bloomberg and Gartner buy massive amounts of data from companies and create news, research, blog posts, and actionable intelligence. Data brokers such as Axiom, Nielsen, and Experian collect data from multiple resources and resell them to marketing agencies and other businesses for a fee.[8]

These businesses curate data and processes, selling them to third-party buyers through a variety of licensing deals. Big companies have the necessary resources to sell and rent data through complex contracting and licensing mechanisms.

In addition to individuals, small companies also give up operational data to centralized platforms without compensation. I bet these companies are even aware of how their data is being sold and resold by the platforms to the highest bidders. Perhaps, some of these smaller companies have no objection to their operational data being sold unless they do not receive compensation for it. These companies want to purposely sell the data and make extra bucks. How do they accomplish this?

At present, data brokers gather data from multiple users through a common platform, aggregate the data, and then sell it. From this, the platform receives compensation from the broker. What about the dozens and hundreds of companies that use the platform? How can the platform compensate these companies whose data was sold to the broker? It

[8]B. Marr. September 7, 2017. "Where Can You Buy Big Data? Here Are the Biggest Consumer Data Brokers," *Forbes.* https://www.forbes.com/sites/bernardmarr/2017/09/07/where-can-you-buy-big-data-here-are-the-biggest-consumer-data-brokers/#34a78ca6c278.

is entirely possible that compensating each company is simply too much work that requires individual contracts, division of payments, and so forth.

What if a data buyer wants to bypass brokers altogether and buy data directly from companies? A key question here is "how can one reduce technical and administrative costs of selling and buying small data sets individually from companies such that it is economically feasible for the buyer to aggregate them afterwards?"

One idea is to allow data sellers to publish the data directly in a decentralized marketplace. The attributes of the data, including licensing rights, are added to a smart contract, which manages the distribution of the fees obtained from buyers. In case the published data is pooled between multiple sellers, then the smart contract knows how to distribute the payment to the data sellers. Figure 10.3 shows a simple concept of data selling and buying enabled by smart contracts. Decentralized means the marketplace doesn't hold the data and instead stays behind the data owner's firewall. Obviously, one of the practical challenges is to determine fair market value of the data being sold in the marketplace.

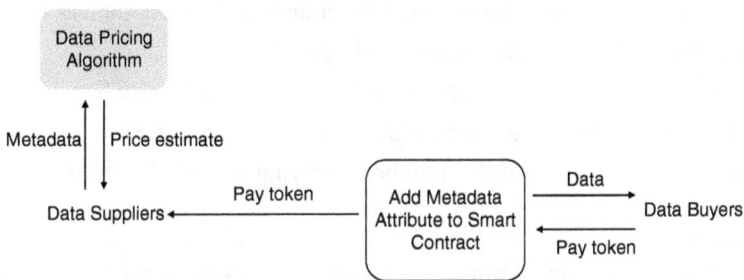

Figure 10.3 Smart contract enables data to be bought and sold in decentralized marketplaces

Ocean Protocol, a Berlin-based startup, has developed a set of protocols that allow companies to monetize data at a much lower administrative cost using smart contract-enforced service agreements. The protocol also includes hashes of metadata and provenance to track who bought the data.[9] Ocean Protocol recently teamed up with Next Billion and Unilever in a new rural retail initiative that provides free point-of-sale platforms to rural store owners in India to record real-time inventory and sales. Stores capture all real-time transactions through the point-of-sale platform. In return, store owners earn additional streams of revenue from Next Billion as royalties for using their data.[10]

Ocean Protocol exposes Next Billion's data assets purchased from store owners, allowing them to be discoverable by potential buyers. This is made possible by registering the data and the associated metadata on Ocean Protocol, with a hashed identification of the data stored on-chain, which links to the asset stored in Next Billion's own premise. Ocean Protocol allows Next Billion to trace a data item back to the sources in case debugging is required. Ocean Protocol extensively utilizes smart contracts called service execution agreements, placed between various steps of data discovery to consumption, to keep track of its provenance.

Invoiceless Payments

According to the American Quality and Productivity Center, the median cost of processing an invoice is 0.08 percent of revenue, which translates into $5.83 per invoice across multiple industries.[11] Other sources have mentioned invoice processing costs as high as $40.[12]

Invoice processing involves not only entering the invoice into a ledger, but also performing cross-verification with contract terms, reconciling with the purchase order number, verifying a sender's information,

---

[9]Disclaimer: At the time of writing, I was working with Ocean Protocol to create a logistics data marketplace for dexFreight Inc.

[10]Ocean Protocol. 2019. "Next Billion and Ocean Protocol Collaborate for a Better Understanding of Asia's FMCG Market," *Ocean Protocol.* https://blog.oceanprotocol .com/next-billion-and-ocean-protocol-collaborate-for-a-better-understanding-of-asias-fmcg-market-9e267ee78601.

[11]"Accounts Payable and Expense Reimbursement Performance Assessment," *American Productivity and Quality Center.* https://www.apqc.org/benchmarking-portal/osb/accounts-payable-and-expense-reimbursement.

[12]M. Palmer. September 7, 2017. "The True Cost of an Invoice to Small Business Owners," *Due Inc.* https://due.com/blog/the-true-cost-of-an-invoice-to-small-business-owners/.

and then issuing a payment. All these tasks require human capital and influence the cost of invoice settlement and payment.

In logistics, the industry I'm quite familiar with, the biggest problem is errors in invoices submitted by a contractor, or carriers. An executive from the largest drayage company in the United States told me that 6 out of 10 invoices that his company receives have errors. Even though the error was a result of the contractor, the company must still spend resources to fix the error before issuing payment to the carriers. The company works with many small, medium, and large carriers as its contractors. Whereas large carriers may have electronic invoicing integrated with the company's systems, small and medium-sized ones often do not.

That means these companies create invoices in a spreadsheet or a word processor and enter invoice amounts manually. The company receives those invoices as e-mail attachments that are then entered into its accounts payable systems manually and reconciled with payment terms and purchase orders. In companies like this, invoice audits and verification may be done by a separate group of individuals that do not have first-hand information of the shipment being processed and whether the shipment has been picked up and delivered and performed to satisfaction as per the contract. In case of any discrepancy, the invoice will be sent back to the original sender for revision.

If both parties have signed a smart contract in which shipment milestones and performance conditions are encoded, then this company doesn't have to wait for the invoice from its contractor. This reduces time to payment. The smart contract can either trigger a bank-to-bank wire transfer or transfer cryptocurrency as payment to the contractor's digital wallet. That means the contractor receives payment faster because there is no likelihood of errors in attributes. However, the smart contract needs to receive information about the milestones and performance from reliable sources. If the contractor performed outside of the defined milestone parameters (e.g., delayed pickup, delayed delivery), then the smart contract needs to have those logics encoded.

One might ask why the company needs a smart contract for this. Why can't they use a web application to sign off an electronic contract and automatically trigger bank-to-bank payment? Yes, this is what companies have been doing for a long time. And it works except when there is a conflict between the parties that requires a third-party audit. Having both parties' performance information on a neutral ledger means the auditing party can quickly verify "what happened" with the shipment without worrying about whether a party has tampered with the shipment information.

The other benefit is the fact that smart contracts can function like an escrow and provide the contractor with milestone-based payments instead of end-result-based payments. Figure 10.4 shows milestone-based payments to a truck as it is moving a shipment, instead of paying the trucking company after delivery. This provides the trucking company with period cash flow necessary to perform its function.

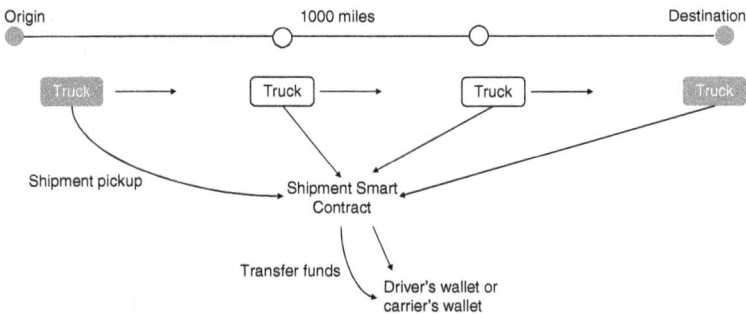

Figure 10.4 Milestone and performance-based frequent payment enabled by smart contracts

This feature really extracts the benefit of smart contracts with real-time milestone-based performance. However, it requires the smart contract to measure the performance quantitatively in real time. Miles driven and other milestones can be easily reported to a smart contract using geo-location devices. There are articles and blog posts (composed for marketing purposes) that say something like "blockchain technology was found to increase efficiency by so and so percentages." But a little investigation will show that such claims lack convincing details about when such conclusions were reached.

Patara Panuparb, a graduate student at MIT in 2019, performed what I think is quite a thorough analysis of real-world supply chain financing benefits of blockchain to four stakeholders in a trade finance

transaction—supplier, funder, buyer, and platform providers.[13] In the supply chain, suppliers are the ones supplying equipment or providing transportation service. A funder is a financial institution that provides liquidity
to the supplier, and the platform provider charges a fee for processing the
invoices and charges a fee to the suppliers. The study found that the use
of blockchain versus blockchain and IoT (13 percent versus 24 percent)
resulted in higher benefits. Another important observation from the study
was that the benefits were not equally distributed between the stakeholders.
In his study, the funder (the bank in his case) was the biggest beneficiary because invoice processing time and cost were significantly reduced by using
smart contracts. Hence, the bank incurred a much lower cost of processing
and funding invoices. The supplier, who received faster funding than traditional processes that did not involve a digital platform, received net zero
benefit because it had to pay high platform fees.

Traceability 2.0

Since the emergence of smart contracts, the supply chain has been mentioned as a low-hanging fruit use case where businesses will implement the
technology. Consultants have written extensively about how blockchain
will revolutionize supply chain and make it more efficient (reference).
Walmart has used the technology to trace the origin of pork (reference),
other use cases. Supply chain is one of those verticals that touch on and
impact everything we do. It is the ultimate backend of global and domestic commerce related to health care, electronic commerce, manufacturing,
finance, and so forth. Hence, it is worth looking at how blockchain im-
proves traceability in the supply chain. It is worth a deep dive.

Traceability 1.0 was achieved using Universal Product Code (UPC)
codes, near-object identifiers such as radio-frequency identification
(RFID), mobile phones, and global positioning system (GPS). Using
these technologies, businesses can tell where a pallet, box, or container is
positioned on earth. Traceability 2.0 means much more than being able
to answer the question "where is it now?"

---

[13]P. Panuparb. 2019. *Cost-Benefit Analysis of a Blockchain-based Supply Chain Finance
Solution* [thesis] (Boston, MA, Massachusetts Institute of Technology).

It also means being able to answer questions such as "where did an object originate from?" "Who approved moving the object along the supply chain?" "Which systems stored information about the object as it moved along the supply chain of manufacturers, distributors, warehouse, and retailers?" Businesses can dig up that type of information, but, as experienced in the case of Walmart, obtaining that information could take days.

Traceability 2.0 is simply this: Enter a UPC code or some form of identification, and in a few seconds the system will be able to tell the entire history of how the object traveled through the supply chain. This has tremendous value in responding to contamination, recalls, and pinpointing the source from where the object first originated, taking necessary actions to stop further contaminations. Other use cases of Traceability 2.0 exist, such as detecting counterfeit goods, detecting stolen goods sold in online markets, and so on.

Traceability 2.0 uses blockchain technology to ensure even the UPC codes or other forms of identification of shipments, pallets are not forged or tampered with on the way. As Figure 10.5 shows, a simple example includes hashing the UPC code along with other shipment attributes and adding to a blockchain. The stakeholders downstream of the supply chain can then verify whether the information matches as they receive the physical goods by comparing the hash in the blockchain.

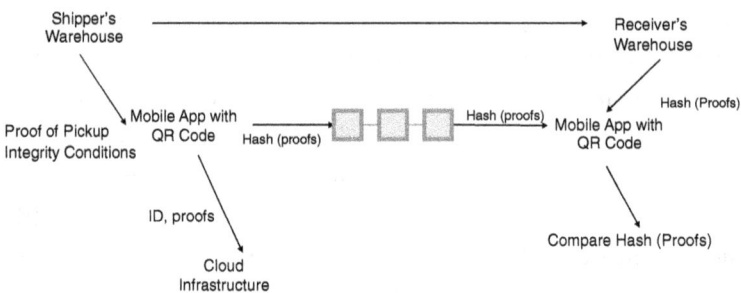

Figure 10.5 Traceability 2.0 that leverages blockchain technology to track shipment provenance

Smart Contract as Escrows

Smart contracts can lock funds until certain conditions are met, and at that point funds can be released to a party mentioned in the contract as a recipient. This is like a traditional escrow service. It is a trusted intermediary between two parties who do not trust each other in a transaction that involves buying and selling goods or services. Both parties sign an agreement to use the escrow service to hold funds on behalf of the buyer and release it at the request of the buyer to the seller. Title companies work the same way when you buy a home. In return, the escrow service charges a fee to the buyer, seller, or both.

A smart contract is provided with the address of the buyer, seller, and the escrow creator. The smart contract itself is typically created by the escrow service. Funds are locked in the smart contract until the buyer sends a message to the contract to release the funds to the seller's address. The buyer also recovers the funds locked in the smart contract if both parties, or the seller individually, cancel the transaction. Essentially, the smart contract can perform almost all the services a traditional escrow service can perform, except make phone calls to the buyer and seller.

As Figure 10.6 shows, at the initiation of the smart contract, it will have a balance equal to 0. The address of the smart contract is the address of the creator or escrow service. After the smart contract receives funds from the buyer, the balance is increased by X, which is the amount received from the buyer. The buyer then tells the smart contract that it is OK to send X to the seller. At that point, the balance is Y equals commission amount, and the seller's balance is increased by X minus Y.

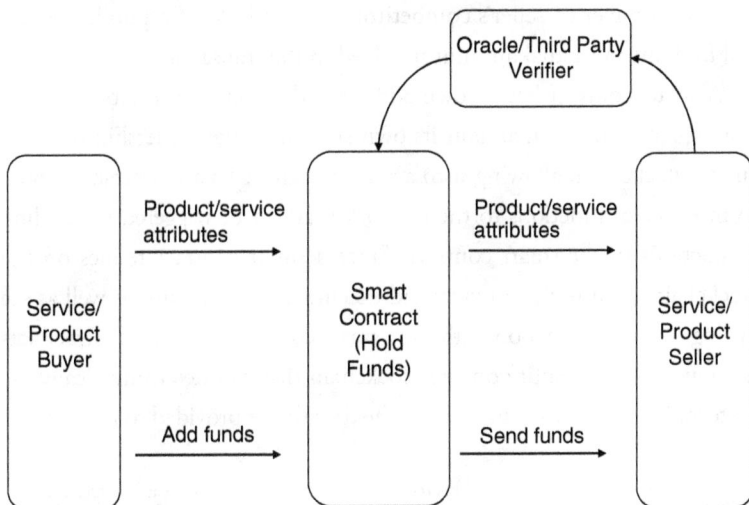

Figure 10.6 Smart contracts can hold, receive, and transfer balances like an escrow service

If the buyer raises a dispute after the funds have been transferred to the seller's balance, then the escrow service provider will have to mediate the claim, and from there on the dispute may even go into arbitration.

It is obvious that developing a real-world smart contract-based escrow service would be much more nuanced and even nontrivial. It will have to include on-chain and off-chain exceptions in handling functions.

OpenBazaar, which is a decentralized p2p marketplace to buy and sell physical merchandise, uses an escrow contract controlled by three signature addresses—with one controlled by the buyer, one controlled by the seller, and one controlled by a moderator that has been agreed on by both the buyer and the seller.[14] In this case, two out of three signatures are required either to transfer funds to a seller or refund back to the buyer. OpenBazaar also allows buyers not to use the moderator to expedite the payment and not to have to wait for the moderator to sign off on the payment.

As pointed out by Steven Goldfeder, from OpenBazaar, involvement of the moderator requires it to be actively involved in every transaction, even when there is no dispute. Second, it is vulnerable to misbehavior by the moderator, which can simply pocket the buyer's payment and never transfer it to the seller if the smart contract is not properly structured and if both buyer and seller are unaware of such an intent. There are also privacy implications of implementing escrow services in public blockchain because the transfer of balances and escrow addresses are recorded. For example, a buyer or seller's competitor may get hold of a public address and find out the actual amount involved in the transaction.

A smart contract has its own address and account on the blockchain. Consequently, it can maintain its own state and take ownership of assets on the blockchain, allowing it to act as an escrow. Smart contracts expose an interface of functions to the network that can be triggered by sending transactions to the smart contract. Since a smart contract resides on the blockchain, each node can view and execute its instructions, as well as see the log of each interaction with each smart contract. A smart contract acts as an autonomous entity on the blockchain that can deterministically execute logic expressed as functions of the data that is provided to it on-chain.

---

[14]A. Williams. October 24, 2018. "Escrow Smart Contract Specification in OpenBazaar," *OpenBazaar*. https://openbazaar.org/blog/Escrow-Smart-Contract-Specification-in-OpenBazaar/.

CHAPTER 11

Creating Innovative Business Models

If we view blockchain as the next generation of ledgers in which transactions, or evidence of transactions, are equally available and accessible to entities involved in those transactions, then this raises the following questions: "What kind of innovative business models can we build on top of this new ledger?" "What kinds of companies will appear on the market?"

If you remember, back in the 1990s and 2000s the Internet economy created highly centralized, winner-takes-all companies. Gennaro Cuofano, the creator of FourWeekMBA, mentioned in a blog post titled "Do Blockchain Business Models Imply A New Business Playbook?" that "[t]he Internet seemed to have produced open business models. However, consolidation kicked in and new 'conglomerates' formed."[1] Mr. Cuofano believes that things will be different this time around because of blockchain.

Mr. Cuofano cites an interesting concept originated by Joel Monegro of the USV venture capital firm. The concept is called "fat protocols theory," in which applications become marginal compared with the underlying protocols, reversing the pattern created by the Internet boom prior to blockchain. The Internet protocols did not store much value, causing us to rely on applications built on top of those protocols to create and store value. In blockchain businesses, because data will be stored at protocol levels and more openly shared, barriers to enter the market

---

[1]G. Cuofamo. "Do Blockchain Business Models Imply A New Business Playbook?", *FourWeekMBA*. https://fourweekmba.com/blockchain-business-models/, (accessed February 23, 2019).

with applications will be reduced, resulting in more collaborative business models rather than centralized, winner-takes-all models.

In "The Truth about Blockchain," Lansiti and Lakhani mention that the same way that TCP/IP dramatically lowered the cost of connections, blockchain could dramatically reduce the cost of transactions. Considering that the core function of any business is keeping ongoing records of transactions, blockchain could reduce the costs of that action. Since ledgers are decentralized and under reliance of intermediaries, they will also result in a lower cost of maintaining trust and hence the cost of doing business.

Tokenization of digital assets is another paradigm shift that will foster innovation. Blockchain allows digital assets to be locked in smart contracts and mint tokens representing the value of the asset without requiring intermediaries and hefty administrative costs. In the section "Tokenization of Nonfungible Assets," I explain how these tokens are minted in smart contracts and ownership of tokens are recorded in blockchain, preventing the double pledging of assets.

If we can tokenize physical assets and distribute tokens so easily without intermediaries or administrative process, I believe this is bound to unlock innovative business models that were simply infeasible and, in some cases, inaccessible in common markets beforehand. Let us look at some of these innovative business models.

Horizontal Resource Sharing

Discussion on asset sharing in this section is not really about Airbnb- or Uber-type asset sharing that we are so familiar with. Rather, I am interested in asset sharing between two or more competing entities deciding to assist each other in closing the short-term resource gap and reducing underutilization of assets. They do so during unexpected events so that the end customer's workflow is unhindered. However, they mention that doing so is clunky, slow, manual, and that most often it does not result in additional profit even though it is necessary to keep their customers happy.

One of my early customers ran a large bonded warehouse inside an airport in Mexico City. There are a total of eight warehouses that receive goods arriving via airplane, store them in the warehouse, and release them at the customer's, or importer's, request. All eight warehouses are separately owned. However, they cooperate, using each other's space. When one company's warehouse reaches overcapacity, they call another warehouse and request space to store a customer's shipments. At the strategic level, they compete for businesses from importers and exporters. At the operational level, during exceptional situations, they share each other's space and moving equipment. This is a typical quid pro quo model.

Another trucking company in Quebec mentioned to me that they share trucks, drivers, and dispatchers with other trucking companies during peak seasons, when demand to move shipments can be overwhelming. No formal agreements exist, and situations are handled on mutual trust built on credibility. We had discussions with the company to use smart contracts to formalize parameters of asset sharing, such as who is being lent assets and whether they are being returned.

A Brooklyn community's solar electricity power sharing as a microgrid is another example of horizontal asset sharing if you consider electricity consumption as an asset.[2] The community has access to a virtual trading platform built on blockchain and allows solar energy producers to sell excess electricity credits from their systems directly to their neighbors in the community without an intermediary.

In all these use cases, asset sharing, physical or electrical, can be done manually or by using a centralized intermediary by maintaining a ledger that is trusted by all participants. However, the cost of maintaining the centralized intermediary is expensive, albeit efficient, and can result in the concentration of power and authority in the hands of whoever has write access to the ledger. The central idea is to instead replace the centralized ledger with public blockchain, even if the intermediary may still exist to maintain the protocols that govern the community in sharing those assets.

If the companies collaborate to the extent that they are sharing their physical resources and operational information, then this practice may be considered "cartels" and "anticompetitive," which many legal jurisdictions

[2]D. Cardwell. March 13, 2017. "Solar Experiment Lets Neighbors Trade Energy among Themselves," *The New York Times*. https://www.nytimes.com/2017/03/13/business/energy-environment/brooklyn-solar-grid-energy-trading.html?_r=0.

frown upon (and rightfully so.) Smart contracts in these formations can be considered "collusive agreements."[3] Hence, this kind of partnership on blockchain (public or private), where the companies are sharing transaction information, should be created only under the watchful eye of legal experts. Hiding transaction details in Merkle trees and digital hashes in a public blockchain may not be enough to avoid legal challenges from government and outside companies.

Fractional Ownership of Physical Assets

In 2018, I authored a report exploring a cross section of blockchain and transportation.[4]

In the report, I described a new form of vehicle ownership that is feasible owing to blockchain and reported that General Motors (GM) and Toyota were working on such projects. In this new vehicle ownership paradigm, instead of a single owner, multiple owners would own or lease a vehicle, making it attractive for a large part of the population that cannot afford to lease cars to do so and share the lease with others.

Owners will utilize smart contracts to define ownership conditions and keep track of accurate mileage and maintenance. Vehicles would be able to upload mileage directly to a blockchain, where transactions will be time-stamped and recorded in immutable blocks for auditing in case of fraud and insurance claims. Public or consortium blockchain can be used where mining nodes provide "proof of movement or maintenance." While working on the report, I interviewed the GM and Toyota executives about motives to build fractional ownership of vehicles. They explained that the reasons behind the motivation were both economic and social. First, vehicles are the second most valuable depreciating asset. Second, the new generation is shying away from owning vehicles.

GM mentioned that it was working on a proof of concept of fractional ownership using its Maven platform. Toyota, through a

---

[3]T. Schrepel. 2019. "Collusion by Blockchain and Smart Contracts," *Harvard Journal of Law and Technology* 33, no. 1, pp. 118-51.

[4]R. Rajbhandari. January 2018. "Exploring Blockchain – Technology behind Bitcoin and Implications for Transforming Transportation - Final Report," *Texas A&M Transportation Institute.* https://static.tti.tamu.edu/tti.tamu.edu/documents/PRC-17-13-F.pdf.

blockchain-mobility.org alliance, is partnering with several startups for a proof of concept that includes an open ecosystem not dominated by a single platform but that is an auto manufacturer agnostic system. In this open ecosystem, any asset owners, as well as auto manufacturers, can put their cars up for rental or fractional ownership. Figure 11.1 shows the concept of using blockchain to store maintenance- related information about cars, including mileage, services performed, and so forth. This is essential for multiple owners of the same car to keep a transparent and immutable information in case they do not share the same insurance and finance companies.

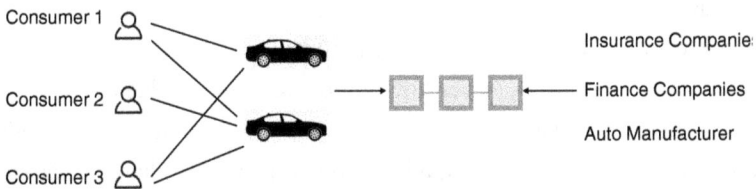

Figure 11.1 Maintenance-related updates about cars are added to blockchain for equal access to insurance, finance, and manufacturers

Multiple individuals and companies owning the same physical asset is nothing new. People have been doing it for centuries. However, it has become rather cumbersome and expensive to properly execute such ownership using complex contractual terms by a title company to de-risk the owners against nonpayments, insurance claims, and other legal issues. Storing usage information in blockchain reduces the administrative cost of maintaining such records and reduces the overhead costs.

Collateralized Lending of Digital Assets

Decentralized lending, or peer-to-peer lending, involves using your cryptocurrency as collateral and obtaining a loan in a different cryptocurrency using a lending platform. A lender loans you the crypto and charges the interest. Until you pay the loan back, your crypto is locked in a smart contract. Once you pay the loan amount plus interest, your collateralized crypto is released back to you. Similarly to the way banks put a lien on your collateral for loan, your crypto is locked in a smart contract, and that is the critical component of crypto lending. The entire process does not require any paperwork, signatures, or credit checks because you are borrowing against your own digital asset. Borrowing against a crypto asset means that the borrower does not have to sell their cryptocurrency.

MakerDAO, BlockFi, and Salt Lending are some of the projects that are pioneering collateralized crypto lending. These platforms allow lending and borrowing on a global scale, something that wasn't possible until now because conventional lending is very much limited to the locations where banks and other financial institutes operate.[5] Crypto lending started in early 2018, and, according to DeFi Pulse, as of December 2019, close to $500 million worth of Ether is locked up in loans.

Also to be noted is that borrowed funds in the borrower's account are in the form of a stable token like or Dai. Otherwise, it wouldn't make economic sense if the price of borrowed funds went up in value by the time the borrower paid back the loan. If the borrower cannot pay the funds back, then the collateral is liquidated. Some platforms allow lenders to change their interest rate and others fix it, which may also depend on collateral, the tenure of the loan, and so forth. Since cryptos are volatile in nature, it may happen that the value of collateral drops beyond a certain level. To protect borrowers in case of a sharp drop in the value of their collateral, the lending platform may allow the margin call, and borrowers can call their loan back.

These lending platforms operate on a smart contract, or a series of smart contracts, which receives the collateral from the borrower and sends the stable coins as funds to the borrower's wallet. Hence, there is little or no paperwork required to issue loans and lock collaterals. Some lending platforms may have another smart contract to liquidate borrower's collateral in case of nonpayment. The smart contract has loan to value, collateralization ratio, and stable coin balance coded into it.

Now the question remains whether it is possible to borrow against noncryptocurrency such as land titles or invoices as collaterals. The

[5]S. Lee. May 22, 2018. "Decentralized Lending Promises Easy and Global Access to Credit, But Is It Too Good to Be True?", *Forbes.* https://www.forbes.com/sites/shermanlee/2018/05/22/decentralized-lending-promises-easy-and-global-access-to-credit-but-is-it-too-good-to-be-true/#6623d0c94c37.

lending platforms described previously use fungible tokens such as Ether and Bitcoin as collaterals.

In the case of uncollateralized lending, a smart contract records the terms and conditions of payments such as principal, interest, and period. A token representing the debt is created and assigned to the debtor. The token is transferred to the creditor, which is recorded in the blockchain. The smart contract then enforces the terms of lending, including payments. In theory, the cost of lending is minimal because it does not involve back office operation to verify identity and a transaction's auditability. However, in practice, such lending still requires credit risk assessment, and KYC checks on creditors and debtors. One obvious benefit is that with little effort, a token representing debt can be split into multiple amounts and sold to creditors.

Land titles and invoices are nonfungible assets. Hence, the first step in borrowing cryptocurrency using smart contracts with nonfungible assets as collaterals is to mint nonfungible tokens (NFTs) with the same value as the value of the asset and then "lock" the asset.

Besides the obvious benefit of tokenization for collaterals, NFTs on blockchain make it easy to track the provenance of the asset throughout the life cycle of the asset. According to Centrifuge's method, shown in Figure 11.2, NFTs are typically created using the ERC-721 standard by combining the public, on-chain data, with a private, detailed

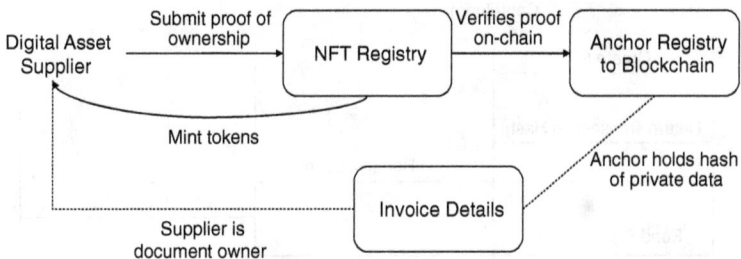

Figure 11.2 Minting of nonfungible tokens against noncrypto assets such as invoices

Source: Recreated from centrifuge.[1]

---

[1] P. Stehlik. July 17, 2018. "Business NFTs — Financial Business Documents as Tokens on Decentralized Networks," *Medium Corporation.* https://medium.com/centrifuge/introducing-business-nfts-financial-business-documents-as-tokens-on-decentralized-networks-ec4b773f7ec5.

representation of each asset that is accessible only by the current holder of the on-chain NFT.[6] Digital asset supplier (creator of invoice) submits the proof of ownership to an NFT registry, which mints tokens equal to the value of the invoice. The NFT registry verifies the invoice details before minting the tokens, which are then used to create liquidity to collateralize the invoice as a noncrypto asset.

The creator of invoice can register the NFT through the on-chain NFT registry by submitting an ownership proof. The NFTs themselves only hold a minimal set of data of the original invoice on-chain to avoid leakage of private data. The on-chain data is used to identify the invoice uniquely and allows anyone to verify the NFTs' data as well as exchange the full invoice data privately within the network.

Subsequently, ERC-20 tokens are minted against the NFTs. Once ERC-20 tokens are minted, all portions of the tokens can be sold off in open or closed markets for the holder of the asset to receive a loan. Some platforms, like Tinlake, also allow NFTs representing invoices to be "pooled" and use them as collaterals. The full process of converting to NFT and minting ERC-20 tokens is shown in Figure 11.3.

Businesses can use collateralized crypto lending, assuming they hold crypto, because they accept it as a form of payment. In the United States,

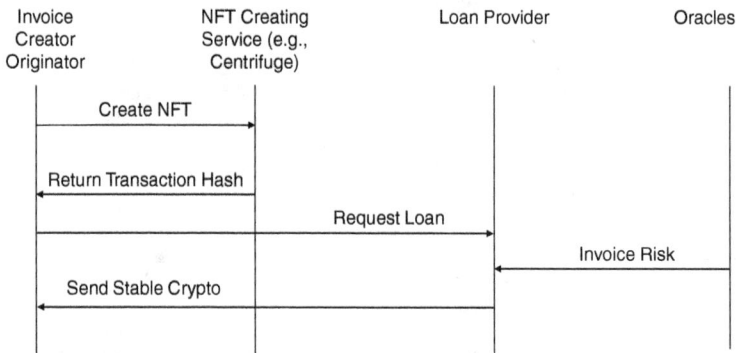

Figure 11.3 Issuing loans against nonfungible tokens representing invoices

---

[6]Centrifuge. May 5, 2019. "Centrifuge: Protocol for Private by Design Transactions on a Decentralized Network," *Centrifuge*. https://staticw.centrifuge.io/assets/centrifuge_os_protocol_paper.pdf.

cryptos are assets, and must hence pay capital gains tax when businesses, and individuals, liquidate those assets. If the price of crypto increases or decreases, while it is locked in a loan, then the business is still liable to report taxes. This may put a huge burden on them during tax filing. On the other hand, businesses can obtain advances or loans against their invoices. Loans are, however, made in stable crypto such as and DAI. Several startups work to factor invoices with much cheaper liquidity than traditional factoring.

Prediction Markets

Decentralized prediction markets built on smart contracts and public blockchain, such as Ethereum, are an interesting concept, because they are based on gambling on silly bets, but for three particularly good reasons. First, they are decentralized, making it unknown how authorities would shut them down. Second, they are borderless, and so anyone in the world can participate in event predictions. Third, these prediction markets have the potential to be oracles to smart contracts and provide information on the crowd-confirmed outcome of events. The second reason is what caught my attention.

First, the prediction market. A prediction market is a place to buy and sell shares in the prediction of future events.[7] There are two types of shares in a prediction market: YES and NO shares. If an event does happen, then people who bought YES shares receive the payout from the people who bought NO shares.

Let us talk about how decentralized prediction markets work. Many of them are already being implemented. I will generalize the workflow based on two projects with the highest market cap—Augur and Gnosis:

1. Somebody starts a bet, or market, for an event. For instance, the Federal Reserve (the Fed) will increase the interest rate on a date.
2. Others participate in the bet by hedging their stake, usually with native tokens. As soon as stakes from both groups, betting for and

---

[7]B. Davidow. April 12, 2019. "The Ultimate Guide to Decentralized Prediction Markets," *Augur*. https://www.augur.net/blog/prediction-markets/.

against, equalize, the bet is closed. In this case, the smart contract that manages the bet is locked.

3. The date of the Fed's decision arrives. The smart contract receives the information that the Fed, in fact, did not raise the interest rate.

4. The smart contract sends tokens to whoever did bet on that outcome, and the smart contract is locked forever, causing its balance to fully deplete.

Decentralized markets operate over public and permissionless blockchain, such as Ethereum with smart contracts, used to send and receive stakes before and after an event has occurred.

Now, there are two assumptions here. The first is that people are not betting for the sake of gambling with 50–50 odds but have done a genuine analysis of why the Fed will or will not raise the interest rate. It is hard to fathom that all of them will do a complicated analysis of possible outcomes, but most will. Second, the oracle that is feeding the actual outcome to the smart contract is, in fact, an oracle and not a fake news website or corrupt data source intending to falsify the outcome.

Once the bet is closed that the Fed did not raise the interest rate, the smart contract that has the information about the actual event can turn itself into an oracle for other decentralized applications. Since several individuals have staked tokens and confirmed that the Fed, in fact, did not raise the interest rate, we can, with great confidence, apply the "wisdom of crowds" theory, which was defined by James Surowiecki's book of the same name. It states that the mean of a large sample of estimates will likely be closer to the true value than most of the individual estimates.[8] Obviously, it holds true if most of the crowd is rational and not colluding to an outcome.

Mark Toner, of ThirtyK, wrote that prediction markets as a source of insights do not require television pundits or "pundit-proof insights" and let them "put money where their mouth is."[9] Allen Farrington believes that prediction markets have the potential to become automated utilities

---

[8]J. Surowiecki. 2005. *Wisdom of Crowds* (New York, NY: Anchor Books).

[9]M. Toner. May 17, 2018. "Prediction Market Could Be Key to Blockchain's Future," *ThirtyK Inc.* https://thirtyk.com/2018/05/17/prediction-markets-blockchain/.

that provide event outcomes with great confidence.[10] Mr. Farrington argues that prediction markets will become an uncorrupted source of truth.

Mr. Toner and Mr. Farrington argued that prediction markets can be used to hedge for and against many future events. Prediction markets remove the counterparty risk to the bookmaker because there is no bookmaker in the first place. That role is replaced by smart contracts with transparency added by blockchain. Furthermore, it will allow individuals and small businesses, with less capital, to hedge against future events, which has been the folly of large corporations, insurance companies, and big banks.

With crowdsourced truth and much like blockchain itself with transactions confirmed using network consensus, prediction markets will provide critical event verification information back to oracles, and smart contract-fueled decentralized applications.

Machine-to-Machine Micropayments

Imagine that your car, truck, or drone has a built-in electronic wallet that can hold, send, and receive money, cryptocurrency, to other machines or services. Imagine a factory full of machines with power to make their own purchases when parts break down. Imagine millions of Internet of Things devices not only sharing data but renting data to each other supported by machine-to-machine (M2M) micropayments. Consider our public infrastructure, including traffic lights, message signs, transit vehicles, and parking meters. These devices we interact with daily have gone through immense transformation over years in terms of their capabilities to perform tasks.

Cars have artificial intelligence (AI) and advanced sensors. Traffic lights have processors with computer vision capabilities and the ability to coordinate among themselves to respond to changing traffic. Factories have sensors and robots with full-on machine learning and AI. The

---

[10] A. Farrington. May 25, 2018. "On Prediction Markets and Blockchains," *Medium Corporation*. https://medium.com/@allenfarrington/on-prediction-markets-and-blockchain-48037d12039d.

amount of computing capabilities packed into these devices is increasing year after year.

One thing these devices have not been able to do is hold, send, or receive money. Yes, you can pay for parking lots or ride a bus using credit cards, but they do not store, send, or receive funds on their own. Devices are not truly autonomous, that is, they don't have economic power, so to speak. Machines are just an interface to collect and send payments. The main reason machines have not been able to autonomously transact payments is that they are not designed to store funds and cannot have a bank account where the payments begin and end.

For the very same reason M2M payments in the context of IoT are still not feasible. Both machines interacting with one another do not have a way to store funds. Moreover, there is the issue of micropayments, which are not feasible, because for banks and credit card companies minimum transaction size is too big for them to be profitable.[11] This limits machines issuing micropayments to other machines without an intermediary intervening to aggregate the payments.

Another example is highway toll payment systems. Every time we pass a toll booth, license plate recognition and radio-frequency identification devices collect license plate and transponder identification number to debit your account. They do not charge a small amount of around $3 to your credit card directly. Tolling agencies will charge your credit card a much larger amount, of around $40, when you've passed the booth multiple times and total charges get close to that minimum required balance of $40. In this example, your car, the transponder, is not paying the tolling agency. Rather, the agency is charging your credit card account.

What if there were a device in the car with the ability to store funds? Every time you pass a toll booth, the agency requests payment to the car and, using the in-built agreement, the tolling agency's machine receives payment directly from the car without the need to use credit or debit cards. What if an automated car can pay a parking spot, a service station, or a fuel station by itself? What if a machine in a factory can order

---

[11]J. Yanowitz. March 13, 2018. "The Future of Micropayments is on the Blockchain," *LinkedIn.* https://www.linkedin.com/pulse/future-micropayments-blockchain-jason-yanowitz.

parts by itself without the need for human intervention? What if it can send and receive micropayments to other machines for providing data, updates, and other detailed information?

It is not difficult to imagine that a whole new economy will emerge if micropayments become the norm. M2M micropayments will revolutionize industries.

Micropayments for M2M payments are feasible with the use of tokens and cryptocurrencies because there are no fixed intermediary fees, only gas fees in the case of ERC-20 tokens. Smart contracts not only facilitate the recording of multiparty M2M transactions but can also be used to enforce contractual obligations between machines. These machines will need wallets and a light node running with persistent Internet connection to interact with smart contracts on the public blockchain to send and receive tokens from other machines.

If tokens solve the M2M payments issue, why hasn't it taken off? There are several challenges that need to be resolved, and I will touch on them briefly:

- Tokens must be accepted at both ends of the transaction, which may be two different companies, bringing up the issue of interoperability of ledgers.
- Administrative costs of issuing tokens, maintaining the ledger, and accounting.
- Float management since tokens and cryptocurrencies function as prepaid stored values different from credit cards.[12]
- Machines need public/private keys with custodial support to retrieve them in case machines are stolen. With billions of devices in use, what does this custodial service look like?
- Although we might think transaction confirmation is slow in public blockchain, the use of state channels such as Lightning can be adequate.

---

[12]Cognizant Reports. November 2015. "Gearing up for Internet of Payments," *Cognizant Reports*. https://www.cognizant.com/InsightsWhitepapers/Gearing-Up-for-the-Internet-of-Payments-codex1549.pdf.

- Microtransactions may not be confirmed by miners and can be delayed compared with large transactions.
- High transaction fees for small or microtransactions (a solution is proposed by Lundqvist et. al.[13])

Crypto-Enabled Automated Machines

Automated cars and trucks are in everybody's mind these days. Automated cars, trucks, drones, and robots are designed to respond to external environments on behalf of their owners. Automated cars/trucks stay in the lane by image recognition of lane markings and radar/lidar to detect nearby objects. Drones find the best path to reach a destination and avoid obstructions in flight. Without AI embedded in those machines, such capabilities would not be feasible. Now, whenever we talk about automation, we think of embedding AI in machines so that they can learn, decide, and execute tasks to respond to outside stimuli and react to the outside environment. AI has made these machines exceptionally powerful.

If we follow the levels of automation (listed in what follows), AI came onto the scene really with automated cars and trucks. We are seeing more and more Level 2 machines available to the public. Level 3 machines are available outside of research labs in very limited scope. Most of them are still at the research and development stage.

Level 0 machine = toasters, refrigerators, garage openers, 1990s automobiles… Essentially, they don't have AI built and are not connected to an external environment.

Level 1 machine = can interact with the external environment and take actions. Machines included are home sensors, partially automated cars, Alexa and Google devices, modern traffic lights, and factory robots. They have limited AI built in as a value add.

---

[13]T. Lundqvist, A. de Blanche, and R.H. Andersson. 2017. "Thing-to-Thing Electricity Micro Payments Using Blockchain Technology," *2017 Global Internet of Things Summit, Geneva.*

Level 2 machine = automated cars and trucks, factory robots, and Boston Dynamics Cheetah-type robots. These machines rely on AI to function.

Level 3 machine = self-sustaining and draw their own energy source. Level 3 machines can define incentives. Think *Star Wars* and *The Matrix*. We are not there yet.

Let us put a crypto wallet on these devices and build some scenarios around what their capabilities and adoption will look like in the future (also shown in Figure 11.4.)

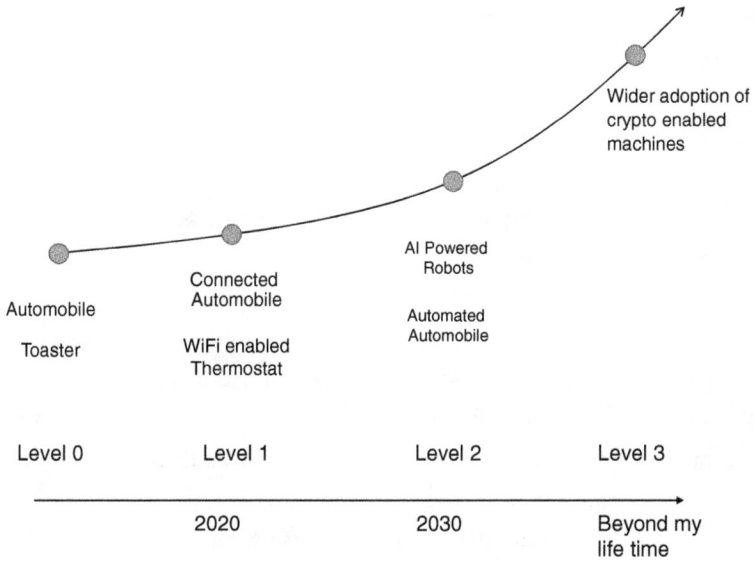

Figure 11.4 Timeline of adoption of crypto wallets

Level 0 = installing a crypto wallet is out of the question because these devices are not connected to the Internet. Wallets need to be constantly connected to the blockchain to reconcile funds transfer.

Level 1 = adding a crypto wallet is possible but infeasible because they are already in the market and the manufacturers may not see much return on investment in adding wallets that connect to blockchain.

Level 2 = these devices are still in the research stage; widespread adoption hasn't happened. They rely to some extent on a persistent Internet connection. They have high-functioning computers, making them an ideal candidate to integrate with crypto wallets. AI can be programmed to manage the wallet. Manufacturers may create value-added services such as part ordering and pay for services.

Level 3 = I believe this level will not exist without the use of crypto wallets and AI to earn and spend tokens at their own will.

Crossover with AI and Machine Learning

Quite a few articles and blogs have been written, describing how blockchain and AI are a "match made in heaven" or how blockchain will provide better data compared with AI models for training. Perhaps oracles that feed data to smart contracts would run on AI to provide better answers. There is a natural synergy between the two technologies because blockchain validates trustworthiness of data while AI requires huge amounts of reliable data to discover patterns and to train models.

However, AI and deep learning have what the experts call an explainability or interpretability problem. Essentially, end users must trust that the models used the right data or right set of data outputs. Instead of AI being a black box, the Department of Defense is working on making AI a glass box with transparency showing each model and how they were used along with a clear audit trail of data between validation and training. This will enable users to rationalize why the AI arrived at a conclusion. Smart contracts can create a pivotal role in keeping an audit trail of data fed continuously into the AI models.

At times we tend to think smart contracts operate in a vacuum. They do not, especially if those smart contracts are to become a ubiquitous mechanism for business transactions. In this scenario, smart contracts may be layered below decision support systems that utilize AI/machine learning to output decision parameters after taking external inputs such as sensor data.

Although AI for the decision support system runs almost independently of smart contracts, they provide valuable services to one another. Alternatively, as Figure 11.5 shows, the smart contract may be encapsulated with the AI, where smart contracts act as enforcers of decisions provided by the decision support system. Hence, the decision support system achieves higher intelligence with AI and financial power with smart contracts.

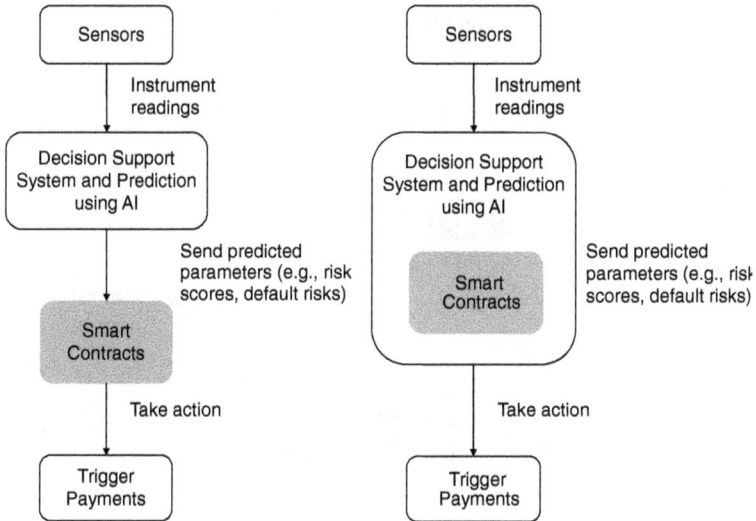

Figure 11.5 Smart contracts may be encapsulated with a decision support system using AI

Another synergy between blockchain and AI is the use of smart contracts to empower processes, or machines, that run AI with money. With AI, these processes become intelligent, but not financially. Smart contracts built into them will dramatically shift that paradigm.

With the ever-increasing power of AI, it is not difficult to see a future where business processes are powered by virtual software agents. These agents can self-modulate as well as possess autonomy and collaboration capabilities. They can learn using AI from past experiences and decide on their own whether to trigger a set of actions. If we are to create a fully or partially automated workflow with minimal human interventions, we anticipate that workflow will be performed by multiple, independent virtual agents collaborating with each other.

The virtual agents will be managed by a coordinating agent on the top of a set of virtual agents, as Figure 11.6 shows. Virtual agents will be connected with blockchain to perform functions such as transfer and receive funds, verify provenance, and so forth. I posit that a human agent will sit on top of the coordinating agent, because our computing ability is exponentially higher than that of any AI available out there when it comes to thinking rationally and utilizing experience in decision making. Human agents will be equipped with a kill switch in case things go wrong and when exceptions must be handled that are beyond the capability of AI within individual agents.

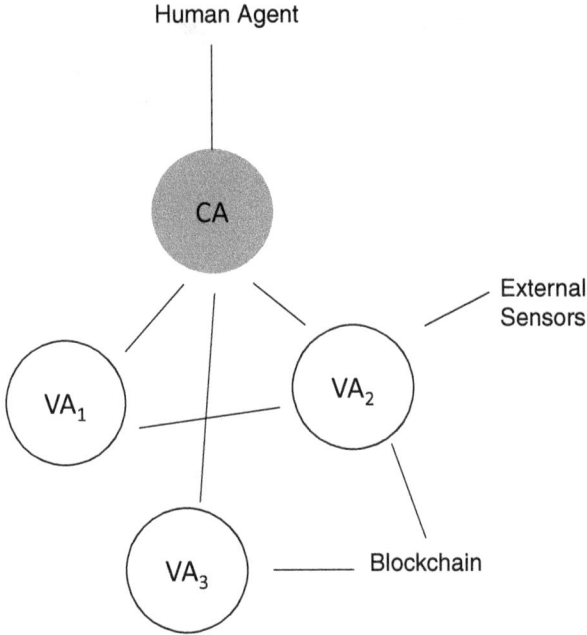

VA = Virtual Agent, CA = Coordinating Agent

Figure 11.6 Humans supervising coordinating agents that manage several virtual agents connected to blockchain

The use of AI in building virtual agents has been going on for decades and is well studied in this space. What I'm projecting is that smart contracts will play a significant role in building virtual agents, perhaps even expediting its development because virtual agents will have the financial power to hold, transfer, and receive funds in addition to other intelligence owing to AI.

Smart contracts are suitable for virtual agents to execute the terms and enforce them with other agents as well as with outside systems. By possessing the ability to transfer funds, the virtual agents will use those funds to buy computing power and other resources such as updating their own AI models or purchasing parts and services.

Blockchain technology can play a role in allowing these multiagent systems to operate in a trustless environment and use the blockchain as an accountability layer—the same way blockchain provided for humans and institutions.

The value proposition of blockchain can be extended to physical devices (e.g., autonomous cars, trucks, robots, drones) that operate as autonomous agents. Blockchain technology provides these devices with fault-tolerant communication, immutable distributed ledger, and, most importantly, a consensus about actions or decisions. By harnessing blockchain's key features, these cyberphysical systems will be able to acquire greater autonomy and independence in jointly performing the required tasks.[14]

Complex Tokenized Systems

Token engineering is the practice of properly analyzing, designing, and verifying tokenized ecosystems.[15] It involves the creation, consumption, and destruction of tokens in a system to align incentives of stakeholders, including actors and parties. The objective of token engineering is to optimize the utilization of tokens to ensure continuous alignment of incentives leading up to maximization of key performance metrics as determined by the stakeholders of the system.

Bitcoin was the first system that utilized underlying cryptocurrency as a token to align incentives of its participants, including consumers, developers, and miners. Consumers consume the token to transfer value, developers maintain the protocol, and miners are rewarded through the creation of new blocks to keep the underlying records tamperproof. Since then, Ethereum and many other public and permissionless blockchains have followed a similar design. We do not, and probably never will, know if Satoshi Nakamoto used optimization techniques to analyze the impact of block rewards and other aspects of the Bitcoin design.

Tokenized systems can be designed with autonomous agents as stakeholders with incentives and disincentives defined by objective functions with constraints. As with any other optimization process, this allows

---

[14]B. Van Lier. 2017. "Can Cyber-Physical Systems Reliably Collaborate within a Blockchain," *Metaphilosophy* 48, no. 5, pp. 698–711.

[15]T. McConaghy.(March 1, 2018. "Towards a Practice of Token Engineering," *Medium Corporation*.https://blog.oceanprotocol.com/towards-a-practice-of-token-engineering-b02feeeff7ca.

designers to perform post optimization analysis such as what-ifs and understanding marginal changes to the system.

You might be wondering why I have included tokenized systems and networks in this chapter about innovative business models. But first, let's talk about incentives and disincentives in traditional business entities and systems. Incentives for stakeholders in multistakeholder businesses, such as two-sided marketplaces, vary depending on whether you are on the supply or demand side. In the case of dexFreight, shippers who need to send a shipment, the incentive is to use the marketplace to lower the cost of shipment. The carrier's incentive is to increase the cost of shipment because their entire revenue is tied to moving those shipments. For the shipper, transportation is a portion of the operating cost.

The keeper's, for example dexFreight's, incentive is to earn fees through monthly subscriptions. Keepers in two-sided marketplaces exist because the incentives of the other two stakeholders are clearly not aligned but need each other for supply and demand. dexFreight's responsibility is to ensure both parties come to an agreement quickly on the transportation price. Because the service does not charge transaction fees, transportation cost that a carrier charges to a shipper are irrelevant to their bottom line even though the usage is higher.

Crypto Asset Staking as a Business

Staking is the process of holding funds in a cryptocurrency wallet to support the operations of a blockchain network.[16] Essentially, it consists of locking cryptocurrencies to receive rewards for work for blockchain such as confirming transactions. Staking originated from the proof-of-stake (PoS) consensus mechanism that many permissionless blockchains use instead of, for instance, proof of work (PoW). Unlike PoW, which relies on mining to verify and validate new blocks, PoS does so with the help of validators who stake their coins. PoS avoids the use of hardware-centric mining and can hence achieve higher scalability than PoW.

---

[16]"What is staking," *Binance.* https://www.binance.vision/blockchain/what-is-staking, (accessed March 20, 2020).

In PoS, validators (or stakers) are chosen randomly although chances of receiving transaction fees and other rewards grow proportionally to the amount of coins they stake.[17] This mechanism also encourages putting users' coins or tokens to "work."

Staking-as-a-Service platforms enable crypto investors to stake their stakable PoS digital assets via a third-party service that takes care of the technical aspect of the staking process. For this service, platforms charge a fee—usually a percentage of the staking rewards.[18] Fees can range from 10 to 25 percent of the reward fee.

Staking is also part of the voting process with a say in the blockchain's governance. The same crypto you hold can be used to obtain rewards for mining blocks and vote on governance. Oddly enough, voting can be about how to increase or decrease the reward. There is a possibility that crypto holders may vote just to increase their reward.[19] Although staking is well intended to "put your money where your mouth is," staking can also lead to entities with the most stake swaying the project's decisions their way although staking is random.

Binance, a crypto exchange behemoth, now has a staking feature offering a list of coins that users can own and hold, earning income as they hold. You can think of it as earning interest on a deposit account. According to Ogilvie, Fenbushi believes staking is one of the "native" and "lucrative" businesses in crypto. Indeed, the staking space is getting crowded with several crypto exchanges and custody firms getting into it. Staked, a staking-as-a-service provider, estimates that annual rewards can go up to $2.5 billion. According to Stakingrewards.com, as of March 2020, $6 billion worth of crypto assets are locked in stakes in various platforms and services.

---

[17]Coinspeaker. January 29, 2020. "Cryptocurrency Staking: Reasons Why Crypto Staking is the New Favorite of Miners," *Coinspeaker*. https://www.coinspeaker.com/cryptocurrency-staking-favorite-miners/.

[18]Blocksocial. January 22, 2020. "Top 12 Staking-as-a-Service Platforms to Stake Your Crypto in 2020," *finivi*. https://www.blocksocial.com/top-12-staking-as-a-service-platforms-to-stake-your-crypto-in-2020/.

[19]J. Yocom-Piatt. June 22, 2019. "Staking Isn't Just a Way to Earn Crypto Money – And It Shouldn't Be," *Coindesk*. https://www.coindesk.com/staking-isnt-just-a-way-to-earn-crypto-money-and-it-shouldnt-be.

Another use case of staking is token-curated registry (TCR), which is a crypto incentivized list (e.g., top restaurants, web contents, reputation) curated by token holders. The token holders are incentivized to maintain a high quality of the list's content, resulting in the demand from the consumers to use the list, which increases the value of the tokens. Candidates or listees in the registry stake tokens to be listed. The token holders may challenge the candidates' contents, and if rejected, the candidate's staked tokens are forfeited and distributed as a reward among token holders who participated in the challenge process.[20]

Token holders who vote for and against the quality of the list also lose their tokens if they side against the majority decision. TCRs challenge many tenets of centralized and traditional forms of lists, in which lists are created, owned, and maintained by an entity. Hence, consumers and candidates must rely on rationale and nonrent seeking behaviors of the list owners. If the list includes some form of ranking, then pay-for-play-type issues arise, by which the highest bidder is ranked high despite the quality it offers.

TCRs sound like oracles—both can be used to ascertain some sort of fact about a state of being. The difference is that the oracles are better at providing objective facts (e.g., temperature today in Seattle), but TCRs are suited for arriving at a consensus about a subjective state using majority voting.

Token-curated marketplaces are a use case of TCRs. Each item listed for sale is a part of a list. The marketplace owner can invite underlying token holders to challenge the quality of items listed by the item sellers. Instead of reviews, the token holders hedge their tokens and vote on quality and other state of the items for sale. TCRs eliminate the fake review problem that has been plaguing so many marketplaces. Existing centralized marketplaces, where moderators ensure the quality of the list items, can be augmented with a tokenized curation process. TCRs are an essential component of decentralized marketplaces because there are no moderators to curate the list. However, I have not come across a marketplace that has utilized the concept of TCR despite potential benefits.

---

[20]M. Goldin. September 14, 2017. "Token-Curated Registries 1.0," *Medium Corporation.* https://medium.com/@ilovebagels/token-curated-registries-1-0-61a232f8dac7.

Perhaps that is because subjective rating of items can go either way even though the token holder may be quite convinced of his or her own rating of an item in the marketplace.

TCRs suffer from practical problems that need to be solved before they become widespread. If the information required by token holders to vote on a topic is difficult to find and/or expensive to acquire, then the token holders may coordinate and collude so that the voting results in their favor.[21] This is where trusted verifiers such as independent reporting agencies, verified buyers, and consumer advocacies will continue to provide a better service than TCRs. In the case of verified buyers, you know that they've bought the item, experienced it, and can provide evidence of issues in the item. The item reviewed by such a buyer is much more convincing than anonymous token holders unless they are also verified buyers of the item. However, in the case of items whose rating or state is inexpensive to determine, it is easy for token holders to determine the rating or state themselves and confidently stake their tokens, resulting in quicker consensus.

---

[21]A. Tabarrok. November 1, 2018. "When Can Token Curated Registries Actually Work?", *Medium Corporation*. https://medium.com/wireline/when-can-token-curated-registries-actually-work-1-2ad908653aaf.

CHAPTER 12

Rise of Decentralized Autonomous Organizations

The decentralization movement picked up speed because of Bitcoin. Decentralized applications, decentralized autonomous organizations, decentralized governance, and more verticals of decentralization, have emerged in the past few years. Irina Bolychevsky, a digital strategist and decentralized technology expert, wrote in her blog post that decentralization is a powerful way to tackle the problems of digital monopolies, growing inequality, and loss of autonomy in our societies. Ms. Bolychevsky also mentioned that decentralization incentivizes the distribution of power across users on the network.[1]

What is a DAO?

Decentralized autonomous organizations, or DAOs, became all the rage in 2016, when the first DAO was hacked, causing Ether to be stolen from its smart contract. This occurrence led to a contentious hard fork of Ethereum to roll back the transaction in the smart contract.

In simple terms, a DAO constitutes ownership agreements that are coded into a smart contract, digitally signed by entities that are part of the project. Such ownership is coded into the smart contract and termed token holders, who hold certain rights and equity in an organization or project. Shares then take the form of tokens. Token holders of the DAO can elect to distribute funds to sponsor other projects or activities.

---

[1] I. Bolychevsky. September 23, 2018. "There's More to Decentralization Than Blockchains and DApps," *Medium Corporation*. https://medium.com/altcoin-magazine/theres-more-to-decentralisation-than-blockchains-and-dapps-35acd2d8f3d6.

Token holders are like shareholders in a company, except that DAOs have no centralized management, as traditional companies do, to govern the organization. In a DAO, token holders govern the project. The question "should DAOs have centralized management or not?" is a subject of debate in the blockchain governance world. We will talk about the governance shortly. A DAO can be something between a traditional corporation and a venture capital (VC) fund or a kick-starter, only entirely decentralized, democratic, and existing only in code.[2]

What Does Governance in a DAO Mean?

Models to govern centralized organizations and systems are well established. Systems are created, operated, maintained, and deprecated under "god" mode, a reference to a core group of directors and managers undertaking such activities while employed by a legal for-profit or nonprofit entity. The core group, along with shareholders, owns the platform, or organization components. In publicly traded companies, shareholders are entitled to voting rights if their stocks are so designated.

Such stockholders can vote on the election of board members, mergers and acquisitions, unionization, and other major decisions that impact the company. In privately held companies, owners and major shareholders basically control all aspects of decision making. Ownership of the entity is clearly separated from users.

The very essence of a DAO is governance, structured in such a way that the power to govern does not rest solely on a single individual or group. Holders of tokens, also called governance tokens or network-generated tokens, have enough power to vote on soft and hard forks to the underlying infrastructure. Holders can also vote on the deprecation or upgrading of components and introduce improvements by way of staking their governance tokens. Such tokens clearly entitle the holders to participate in governance defined in the DAOs' bylaws encoded in smart contracts.

---

[2]S. Bannon. May 16, 2016. "The Tao of "The DAO" or: How the Autonomous Corporation is Already Here," *TechCrunch*. https://techcrunch.com/2016/05/16/the-tao-of-the-dao-or-how-the-autonomous-corporation-is-already-here/.

Governance in DAOs ensures that separation of users, developers, and miners is blurred and that incentives are aligned among the three.

On-Chain and Off-Chain Governance

An example of on-chain governance includes token holders voting or hedging their stake on improvements such as proposals or forking, brought forth by users, miners, and developers. Results of the vote, along with the public keys of voters, are recorded on the blockchain to sustain a fully transparent election. An example of off-chain governance includes Bitcoin Improvement Proposals (BIP) brought forward by anybody in a mailing list-type system. Miners, nodes, and users all can revolt against the improvements and forks. However, there are no elections, and nobody must stake their holdings in support of a proposal.

Sybil Attack During On-Chain Elections

In a traditional public company, individuals are constrained to vote multiple times by validating their identification, issued by a centralized authority. In decentralized blockchains, such as Ethereum, there is no such thing as an individual, only private and public keys. This can lead to Sybil attacks because an individual can create hundreds of private and public keys and vote on-chain to influence the outcome of an election.

Low Participation Problems

The subject of on-chain versus off-chain is currently up for debate and research. One school of thought holds that in the early stages of the project, a centralized management in the form of core developers, governed by off-chain governance, is important to sustain the project, while other token holders take part in electing delegates or direct voting of proposals. Another school of thought holds that the project should be fully governed only by token holders, irrespective of who they are, and the project is sustained by awarding work to individuals and groups who maintain or improve the project.

Kill Switch and Escape Hatch

In case a DAO is attacked, or a major flaw detected in the smart contract code, the creator of the contract may find it beneficial to simply kill the contract and create a new one. This means entities cannot interact with the old one anymore, and the contract is rendered useless. Because smart contracts are created by a single address, or multisig address, they are the only ones that can kill or stop the contract's operation. An escape hatch is simply a mechanism to stop the operation of a smart contract until it is fixed.[3]

A kill switch, in a DAO, opens multiple issues and even dilemmas. First, the activation of the kill switch by the contract creator at their free will is against the ethos of decentralization and autonomy and also against the wishes of the token holders in the contract because the contract owner is like a centralized intermediary. The second issue is that because the contract creator may be held liable for ramifications following the killing of the contract he or she may refuse to kill it.

The third issue is that the kill switch may be subject to theft, misplacement, or malicious activity by bad actors.

Nonetheless, implementing a kill switch might be necessary during the early stages of contract deployment when bugs have not been fully revealed to the developers.

Can a DAO Exist in Its Truest Meaning?

I would argue that Bitcoin is closest to a DAO in its truest sense. It operates in its own environment, free of organizational hierarchy or even fiduciary duties tied to individuals or corporations. Ethereum comes in close second because the Ethereum Foundation still exerts some control over the fate of the ecosystem. The Ethereum Foundation does not have a kill switch to Ethereum, but it owns a sufficiently large portion of Ether to influence the direction of the protocol.

Other DAOs do not even come close to these two, although that does not mean they will not come close sometime. What I have learned is that

---

[3]I. Eyal and E. Sirer. July 11, 2016. "A Decentralized Escape Hatch for DAOs," *Hacking Distributed*. http://hackingdistributed.com/2016/07/11/decentralized-escape-hatches-for-smart-contracts/.

people, in general, tend to believe you when you say that your thesis is to ultimately become a DAO and that you have a path to get there.

Over the next few years, we will see many forms of DAOs, and that is perfectly fine. As with any other strong paradigm to be adopted, it must go through a long evolutionary process. The current generation of DAOs are mostly built on Ethereum and supported by a nonprofit foundation, raising funds using a variety of token-generation events. The foundation then assigns a portion of the funds raised to continue to support protocol development and fund the ecosystem. The foundation is governed by on-chain or off-chain governance of token holders along with a group of individuals taking fiduciary roles to run a legal entity. However, token holders are provided with opportunities to vote for minor and major improvements to the protocol.

For example, MakerDAO's token holders make decisions by staking their tokens to set stability fees as well as the inclusion of collaterals in algorithmic minting of DAI tokens. However, in the case of Maker, only a handful of DAI token holders participate and stake their tokens in the decision-making process. One might argue that because it requires the participation of humans in determining the stability fees instead of using smart contracts, MakerDAO is a "simulated" DAO. I, however, would argue that they are an inspiration to many other would-be DAOs. They are set up in many ways to be a smart contract-only-enabled DAO that will eventually use minimal human intervention to set stability fees.

Anybody intending to create a DAO will encounter a serious, nontechnical dilemma, namely, whether to make it a legal entity or not. Assuming you have resolved the issue of how to structure the smart contract to release tokens, fund projects, and be governed, the dilemma remains. Without giving it a legal structure, raising tokens to fund projects might be considered raising investments in the eyes of major jurisdictions. For example, the Securities and Exchange Commission (SEC) has made it clear that funds raised through what it calls "virtual organizations" with expectations of profit are still considered securities and hence federal securities laws are applicable.[4]

Giving DAO a legal structure is costly in terms of legal fees to comply with regulatory and incorporation laws. When you incorporate a legal

---

[4]Securities and Exchange Commission. July 25, 2017. "SEC Issues Investigative Report Concluding DAO Tokens, a Digital Asset, Were Securities," *Securities and Exchange Commission.* https://www.sec.gov/news/press-release/2017-131.

entity, someone still must be registered as the legal owner of the registered entity. Along with that come the fiduciary responsibilities of running it. From there, the relevant question is "how is this a 'decentralized' entity?"

DAO maximalists need to understand that DAOs are as good as the extent of the certainty encoded in smart contracts. Obviously, there are no perfect or complete smart contracts, or traditional contracts, with every contingency possible. It is naïve to think that future decisions and contingencies associated with those decisions can be appropriately encoded in smart contracts. That is why a truest DAO will not and should not exist. Nonetheless, I do believe forms of "DAO lite" will exist and greatly benefit business models that provide public utility infrastructure.

A true form of a DAO won't exist because a complete contract, which is a precursor to a true DAO, would make ownership of assets irrelevant since incomplete contracts would not have residual rights of control of those assets.[5] McAfee and Brynjolfsson even wrote in their book, *Machine Platform Crowd*, that they are pessimistic that DAOs will ever be economically dominant because smart contracts will not replace management. Management functions and has value because perfect contracts are difficult, if not impossible, to construct.[6]

Misguided Push to DAOs

Bitcoin is one of the black swan events in technological history. It will be long before an innovation like Bitcoin occurs. It will take decades for another Ethereum-type network to be discovered. It will be years, perhaps decades, before a truly decentralized system will emerge and become mainstream. I would like someone to prove me wrong and make it happen sooner.

Cryptocurrency venture capitalists and investors in 2017 and 2018 were all strung out on decentralization. They said they invest only in decentralized projects with cool protocols and wanted tokens in the DAO. To my and my colleagues' surprise, I was told the same thing by

---

[5]S.J. Grossman and O.D. Hart. 1986. "The Costs and Benefits of Ownership: A Theory of Vertical and Lateral Integration," *Journal of Political Economy* 94, no. 4, pp. 691-719.
[6]A. McAfee and E. Brynjolfsson. 2017. *Machine Platform Crowd* (New York: W. W. Norton & Company Inc.)

cryptocurrency investors. For us, it felt immature that these investors were promoting decentralization and DAOs more than the product-market fit.

In late December 2019, Jesse Walden from Andreessen Horowitz, a renowned VC firm, wrote in a blog post that decentralized applications should first focus on product-market fit and worry about decentralization in later stages of applications built on blockchain.[7] From then on other investors followed suit. I knew that the misguided push to decentralizing applications first was going to fall apart because if the product is not ready for users, what good does the decentralizing do? There were also issues about legalities surrounding true DAO organizations that cannot exist by meeting the legal requirements of jurisdictions like the United States.

DAO as a Public Utility Infrastructure

Projects such as Ethereum, MakerDAO, Ocean Protocol, Aragon, and even Bitcoin in many ways, function as a community-owned public utility infrastructure. In our daily lives, local roads and highways, water supply lines, and stormwater drainpipes are examples of publicly owned utilities. They are built and maintained largely by taxpayer funds. We, the taxpayers, contribute to their maintenance through sales, real estate, and income taxes we pay to federal, state, and local governments. No single individual or company owns these utilities. In the same way, no single individual or company owns the Bitcoin or Ethereum network. Every time we use their underlying infrastructure to send bitcoins or create smart contracts, we pay fees that keep that infrastructure operational via mining nodes.

Most DAOs are structured as nonprofits without centralized and concentrated ownership by a single person or entity, much like our public utility. As Figure 12.1 shows, there are core developers that build and maintain the underlying infrastructure. The DAO may assign such responsibilities to a private company. A governance team consisting of token holders decides through open voting system on upgrades and forks. The infrastructure is typically open for everybody to participate, contribute, and build applications.

---

[7] J. Walden. January 9, 2020. "Progressive Decentralization: A Playbook for Building Crypto Applications," *Andreessen Horowitz.* https://a16z.com/2020/01/09/progressive-decentralization-crypto-product-management/.

Users
App Developers   DAO   Core Governance   Core Developers   Infrastructure

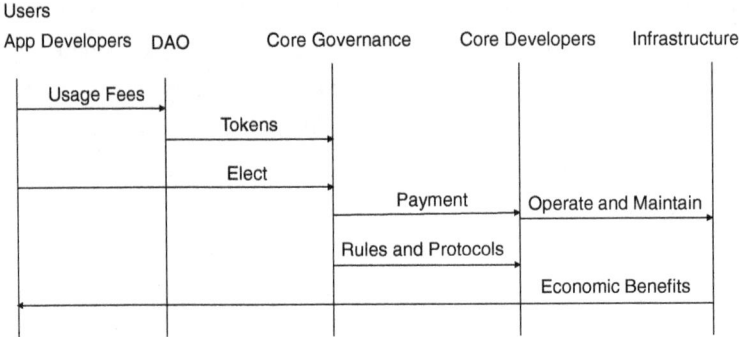

Figure 12.1 Typical structure of a decentralized autonomous organization

DAOs that cannot be structured as for-profits to issue security tokens can instead be structured as nonprofits and sustained by members or stakeholders paying "tax" for using the infrastructure. Just as municipalities and counties borrow initial capital to build those highways, DAOs can be initially funded the same way and maintained by charging "tax" to users. In the case of Ethereum, that "tax" or "toll" is the gas fees. In this case, with the DAO being a nonprofit, it pays dividends and/or distributes profit to the bondholders until maturity.

Why Should Traditional Businesses Care?

DAOs can present a clear challenge in the future to traditional business models consisting of centralized power and a hierarchical structure of governance. The concept of DAO is so novel that in the larger scheme of things it has not defined the extent to which DAOs challenge traditional businesses.

An entity that is owned by multiple contributors in the form of token holders, such as ICO's, since inception, may create a much quicker network effect in terms of scaling the operation than a traditional bootstrapped or investor-backed entity because those contributors can act as influencers and end users. However, the entity must prove the value proposition and product-market fit in the case of novel ideas and previously nonexistent business models.

In the previous section, I talked about DAOs as a public utility built either as a general purpose or as a domain-specific infrastructure. The utility provides a neutral platform for stakeholders to operate on and acts as a bridge between competing stakeholders. There are many examples of entities created and sometimes owned by industry consortiums. Examples of such entities are GS1 in supply chain, SWIFT for interbank data transfers.

Syndicates exist that work on behalf of their members and act as market makers by defining market prices. Syndicates may be for-profit or nonprofit, financially sustaining themselves by either charging members for transactions they process on their behalf or through membership fees. What makes DAOs any different from the preexisting neutral platforms is the fact that DAOs mostly operate out of smart contracts where operational transactions are managed in public blockchains. Why should anyone bother to build a DAO instead of a traditional for-profit or nonprofit? The reason is that a good many legal mandates to create and operate such entities already exist.

DAOs have the potential to operate on significantly quicker funding using crowd sourcing and ICOs, lowering operational costs by using smart contracts. They also operate on a much higher level of transparency when it comes to use of funds, whether that is to distribute dividends, award projects, or pay salaries to developers.

CHAPTER 13

Selling Blockchain as Other Than Blockchain

The Economist ran a cover story back in 2015, calling the technology behind Bitcoin a "trust machine." Nothing can be further from the truth. Blockchain is a machine that will lower the cost of trust in trade and economy of $23 trillion.[1] Blockchain is a trust layer for platforms and applications. It is a trust protocol for networks. It is not a database layer or a storage layer. In fact, blockchain doesn't perform well in any of those areas and was never conceived to be either of the two. It is a ledger, a truth ledger, that stores transactions between two parties, two machines, two human beings, or two enterprises anywhere in the world.

> *With the possibility of reversal, the need for trust spreads.*
>
> *—Satoshi Nakamoto*

All blockchain does is record who gave what to who and when. That is all it does. How can such a simple concept be so powerful? The simple answer to that simple question is that all we do every day is give and take something to and from somebody else. It may be physical goods, information, data, algorithms, reports, e-mails, songs, money, and many others.

That is what commerce consists of. It runs on manufactured trust. Did you notice that the first word in Satoshi Nakamoto's famous white paper is the word "commerce"? Trust is foundational to commerce, trade, supply chain, and lemonade stands. Yet maintaining trust is expensive,

---

[1]S. Davidson, M. Novak, and J. Potts. July 24, 2018. "The $29 Trillion Cost of Trust," *Medium Corporation*. https://medium.com/@cryptoeconomics/the-29-trillion-cost-of-trust-be8ffbd5788d.

time-consuming, and inefficient. It seems ironic that as digital transforms the world, one of its more promising building blocks is a throwback to our decidedly analog past.[2]

In every transaction, trust is essential. I would not buy lemonade from a kid if I did not trust him or her. Sometimes I do take a risk and forget about trust because I'm super thirsty. But that is rare. The second part of trust is verification. If I am buying lemonade, then before paying for it I will ask if they are from the neighborhood, and if so which house, and which school he or she attends. Asking those questions is another means of verifying trust.

Companies similarly verify trust by ensuring the counterparty has the appropriate documents such as social security, permits, insurance and line of credit. For being a trusted third party, government agencies, insurance companies, and banks are paid commissions. Increasingly, if you have not noticed, trusted third parties have started to encroach on customers' identity and privacy. The worst case is attempted control of the market.

Blockchain as an Evolution of Ledger

One of my favorite things when explaining blockchain to businesses is to describe blockchain as a new kind of ledger, perhaps an evolution of the ledger. From early clay tablets to Sumerion cuneiform tablets in 7000 BC to double-entry accounting systems around 1300, AD ledgers have evolved in a way that has arguably changed trade, supply chain, banking, and other aspects of the market.

Fast forward to the 1960s. With the advent of computers, and later the World Wide Web, we saw digital banking in which accounts receivables, debits and credits, and ledgers became digitized. From there, ledgers evolved into spreadsheets, relational databases, and web-based read and write databases. The last one contributed to global electronic commerce.

Not only banks, but governments too started to maintain digital ledgers with transactions about property transfers, voting records, stock

---

[2]E. Piscini, J. Guastella, A. Rozman, and T. Nassim. August 31, 2016. "Blockchain and the Democratization of Trust," *The Wall Street Journal.* https://deloitte.wsj.com/cio/2016/08/31/blockchain-and-the-democratization-of-trust/.

transfers, and more. Banks started to maintain ledgers for the financial transactions of its depositors. Individuals maintained ledgers in personal computers and later in servers and cloud-based applications.

Hence, ledger-recorded entries became a digital representation of assets. Ledger entries in banks became money,[3] which also became a centralized system of trust, allowing people who didn't know each other to trade and exchange goods.

When blockchain introduced the concept of decentralized ledgers, it also challenged the centralized system of trust and our overreliance on a trusted central authority and powerful intermediaries, or keepers of the ledgers. Bitcoin exemplified how ledgers, distributed over multiple independent nodes and secured using clever cryptography, made it possible for decentralized trust. Ledger entries became a digital representation of assets but without banks' involvement.

Similarly, the evolution of centralized ledgers, for lack of better a phrase, facilitated and revolutionized modern-day trade and finance. The question we should ask ourselves is "what kind of opportunities will the decentralized ledgers create?"

Do Not Sell Blockchain, Sell Transparency

A few months back, I was invited to present blockchain 101 to a group of firms and government agencies moving containers in and out of a maritime port in Mexico using ships. The business innovation manager at one of the terminals at the port articulated his vision of how blockchain technology could potentially improve port operations.

The process of loading and unloading a container onto and off a ship involves brokers, port operators, port authority, federal and state government, an exporter, an importer, a trucking company, and so forth. The process is subject to numerous oversights from national government agencies such as federal tax authorities and customs agencies.

Government must make sure each container contains goods that can be exported and imported and that proper tax and duty has been paid.

---

[3]LLFOURN. February 15, 2018. "A Brief History of Ledgers," *Medium Corporation*. https://medium.com/unraveling-the-ouroboros/a-brief-history-of-ledgers-b6ab84a7ff41.

Even within government, there are agencies, each with a different scope of oversight over what can be exported and imported. Then there are customs agents working on behalf of exporters to fill out paperwork requesting the government to let them load the container. The terminal operator must then make sure the container has been sealed and authorized by the government. If an incident occurs, then insurance companies and banks may get involved as a provider of credit or lien holder on the container.

In brief, after I finished blockchain 101 and explained the power of collaboration, senior executives of the port said that we see the power of blockchain is increasing efficiency and accountability by forcing the stakeholders to be about who did what in the process of loading or unloading containers. Light bulbs went off in everybody's head in the room. They said, "We can create a platform where all the agencies are part of a circular network with no hierarchy, making it a flat, circular network."

It was clear from the workshop that blockchain was not about creating an application to prevent agencies from entering misinformation but about holding them accountable for entering that misinformation and then collaborating to prevent it from happening. That is what transparency in the network does. It holds individuals and agencies responsible for irresponsible behavior.

At the same time, the participants should also be rewarded for being part of this transparent network. The reward to the port community in this case was being able to reduce the container export/import process from 4 hours to 1 hour, saving the agencies millions of dollars in customer service and back-office operations.

You must remember that blockchain technology is not about preventing wrong or erroneous information from being added by participants in the network. It is about creating a network with a shared ledger by which individuals are held accountable when that happens and discouraging them from doing so by instituting a penalty.

Blockchain is a counterintuitive, albeit new, form of transparency.[4] It is new in that transparency in the past has been achieved through nondisclosure agreements and gentlemen's agreements. Sharing an electronic

[4]Dgwbirch. July 15, 2018. "Supply Chains and Blockchains," *Medium Corporation.* https://medium.com/@dgwbirch/supply-chains-and-block-chains-980a7340bcbd.

ledger is unheard of and is hence also counterintuitive. Paul Martyn claimed, "Collaboration through distributed databases will make the supply chain more transparent," as an inevitable event. Mr. Martyn thinks that companies should get on board to avoid consumer liability, because that is inevitable too.[5]

Blockchain Is a Risk Management Tool

Blockchain's key value propositions of immutability, no single point of failure, and tamper resistance have implications of risk reduction for individuals and businesses alike. Bitcoin, and other cryptocurrencies, has proven to be a reliable means for individuals to transfer fungible assets without the need for intermediaries, which can be compromised or can create price barriers. For businesses, risks exposed by third-party intermediaries can be alleviated by using smart contracts. Businesses that are highly dependent on intermediaries can gradually and completely wean themselves off by using decentralized platforms, distributed applications, and smart contracts.

Intermediaries are a point of risk on a value chain. However, this is far from being a black-and-white issue. Many intermediaries provide services to their customers who, among other things, lack the expertise or resources to aggregate information, choose from multiple providers, or negotiate on behalf of insurance brokers. There are also issues related to outright fraud and scams that blockchain has the potential to eliminate. However, this requires horizontal collaboration with companies.

In 2014, companies controlled by a Chinese-born Singaporean businessman were alleged to have used invoices for the same metal stockpiles several times to defraud Standard Chartered of $200 million. In 2008, a similar incident involving fictitious purchase orders and fake invoices cost banks, including JPMorgan Chase and Co., close to $700 million.[6]

---

[5]P. Martyn. March 28, 2018. "Does Blockchain Provide the New Standard for Transparency?" *Forbes*. https://www.forbes.com/sites/paulmartyn/2018/03/28/does-blockchain-provide-the-new-standard-for-transparency/#300af0093921.
[6]C. Chanjaroen and D. Boey. May 23, 2016. "Fraud in $4 Trillion Trade Finance Turns Banks to Digital Ledger," *Livemint*. https://www.livemint.com/Industry/CXfxl1yePlwTDuokXU3c2K/Fraud-in-4-trillion-trade-finance-turns-banks-to-digital-le.html.

The same news outlet reported that Standard Chartered, and a few other banks, are experimenting with a blockchain-based solution in which details from an invoice are used to generate a unique hash value stored on the ledger, which appears if another bank tries to register the same details separately. This prevents someone from borrowing multiple times against the same invoice from more than one financial institution. It also allows the financial institutions to prevent fraud without sharing personal identifiable information about the person.

Businesses that receive invoices from hundreds of vendors and contractors have teams of auditors and accountants reconciling these invoices before issuing payments. Every incoming invoice is scrutinized. One executive asked me, "Why isn't there a system by which only troubled or suspicious invoices are scrutinized instead of all of them?" The rest of the low-risk invoices are automatically issued payments. The executive was hoping the blockchain technology would allow that to happen one day.

Sharing Threats and Risks

One of the use cases of blockchain and the ethos of collaboration through a shared, immutable, tamperproof ledger is sharing threats and other risks with peer companies. I am no expert on this topic but was introduced to these risks by folks I know at a few Fortune 100 companies.

These acquaintances asked for my views about what it would take for companies to collaborate to reduce the time and costs of onboarding vendors and subcontractors. An auto company executive I talked with mentioned that they spend millions in vendor management. Every time a new vendor is onboarded to supply materials, they must go through a tedious process of due diligence about the vendor. He said, "Wouldn't it be great if we can create a decentralized vendor management system with participation from auto companies and reduce duplicate effort of due diligence"? I said, "Aren't there already companies and platforms that provide these kind of services"?

He said, "Yes, but we are getting secondhand information. I would rather get firsthand information from another auto company about the vendor." Frankly, I have no idea what it would take to build such a system, but it seems like it's worth an effort. Beyond implementing this concept in blockchain, there must be a massive legal implication in case a peer company falsified information about a vendor.

The second use case, as described by a system engineer at a large logistics company, was sharing threat intelligence. As it happens, they are constantly battling cyberattacks from state and nonstate actors. During that process, they have built a database of IP addresses where such attacks originated from. I am sure this is much more nuanced than what I mentioned. His question to me was remarkably like the question by the auto executive. I am sure there are cybersecurity companies and consultants who keep records of these threats. The answer from the engineer was like the one from the auto executive, "I'm getting secondhand information from the consultant and can't verify if those Internet addresses are a threat. I would rather get that information from our peer company."

Building a collaborative network where companies share risks and threats is not trivial. This kind of collaboration requires changing the paradigm from "privileged vs. the cyber threats" to "us vs. the cyber threats" in the future.[7] This is not a blockchain problem but a human problem.

Outsource Risk and Trust to a Network

If you use decentralized networks to transact with other parties, it would be fair to say that the network is assuming the risk of such transactions, instead of a third party or intermediary. If you transfer Bitcoin to a friend, then the network and the protocol are assuming the risk of transfer. While sending funds from one bank to another, banks and other intermediaries assume the risk of such transfer. Assuming they take responsibility in case of failure to transmit, you may get the money back. If the Bitcoin network crashes, hypothetically speaking, in the middle of the transfer, most likely you will not get it back. The network may hard fork and give the Bitcoin back, but that is very unlikely.

If you use a decentralized platform built on Ethereum, for example, where smart contracts hold transactions that record asset transfers, then

---

[7] R. Shahare. March 02, 2019. "Blockchain, for Threat Intelligence Maybe?", *CPO Magazine.* https://www.cpomagazine.com/cyber-security/blockchain-for-threat-intelligence-maybe/.

you are essentially outsourcing the risk to the Ethereum network. If your customer complains that the asset transfer you initiated over the Ethereum network did not occur, then you cannot call Ethereum customer service, because it does not exist.

Although these are disadvantages of outsourcing trust and risk to a decentralized network, there are also many advantages. The first is that doing so would result in significant cost savings because you do not need to build complex infrastructure to store transactions or resources to secure them.

The question remains: "How long will it take for us to fully trust a decentralized network to hold our assets and outsource risks to these networks?" We still store files in hard drives and in printed form instead of in the cloud.

CHAPTER 14

Overcoming FOMO and Nudging Companies

A medium-sized trucking company out of Memphis told me they want to do something in blockchain because the customers have been posing the question "what are you doing with blockchain?" A port operator in Mexico called me about blockchain when at a meeting with CEOs from several ports one of them brought up the subject of blockchain and nobody knew what to say. I have found through them that innovative companies do not like to say *we do not know* when their customers enquire. They like to say, instead, "We'll find out." Perhaps that is what sets them apart from the rest of the pack.

It is important to manage their expectations and take them out of the hype. It is also important to be truthful and objective about what blockchain can and cannot do. It is important to say, "No, it will not solve all your problems in every department of the company."

I have found that companies can best be helped to overcome fear of missing out (FOMO) through the following three-stage process: blockchain 101, stakeholder workshops, and proof of concept.

Blockchain 101, which I have held dozens of times, helps companies, especially leadership, to understand how blockchain technology works at a high level. It explains how key components of blockchain work together, including ledger, consensus, network, and cryptography. Most importantly, it describes how it helps entities work in a collaborative environment. In most instances, companies will start ideating about how and where it can be applied. Blockchain 101 is the first step in managing their expectations and getting them out of the hype mentality.

Stakeholder workshops help companies identify specific workflows that will benefit from blockchain. Workshops also help companies identify specific blind spots in their workflows. You may need to hold more than one workshop—one with counterparties, another with the departments concerned, and so on.

Proof of concept is an inexpensive way of finding out whether blockchain will fix the blind spots identified in a workflow. It provides parameters for stakeholders to decide how they want to implement blockchain—integrate with their existing system or create a new one. The proof of concept provides implementation options and understands the feasibility of individual options.

Meet, Greet, and Understand Pain Points

The biggest disrupter of blockchain is trust. It will usher in a new era where individuals, machines, and companies, who do not trust each other, share goods and services. It will allow them to create mutually beneficial networks that will function on blockchain as a trust layer. It will allow businesses to lower the cost of maintaining and verifying trust, lowering, in turn, the cost of commerce.

The technology allows individuals and businesses to verify their attributes without disclosing evidence or government-provided documents. Companies can verify whether a counterparty has adequate insurance without asking for insurance documents. Verifying counterparty documents and identification will be frictionless, and that means that settling transactions will also be frictionless.

Every industry sees the potential of blockchain and how it can be applied in their business differently. When I presented blockchain 101 to furniture retailers, one of them, a large retailer, said they wanted to use it in their accounts department to reconcile and settle invoices quickly and with less resources. I never heard that before. It made perfect sense because this company receives invoices from hundreds of suppliers around the world. Before issuing payments, they must dedicate resources to reconciling each agreement, identities of suppliers, invoices, and actual deliveries.

Another group of individuals wanted to create a nonhierarchical community system engaged in moving goods in and out of the maritime port in Mexico. They wanted to create a truly transparent system where everybody contributes information and collaborates, reducing friction while moving containers in and out of the port. Before I told them about blockchain technology, they were struggling to define the system. For them, blockchain technology and consensus protocols are a tool for accountability.

A transportation engineer that I met at an automated vehicle symposium told me he wanted to create an ad hoc network for intersections where automated vehicles do not collide with each other or hit pedestrians. In the network, vehicles will be incentivized to share information with each other using blockchain as a trust layer.

A startup in California wants to use blockchain and cryptocurrency to monetize the habits of viewers, allowing viewers to sell that information to movie production companies. It will allow viewers full control of what kind of viewing habits to sell and, most importantly, without exposing their personal identifying information.

A trucking company executive out of Montreal, whom I met at the Blockchain in Transport Alliance conference, told me he wanted to create a network of other trucking companies in the area to share their resources such as drivers, trailers, and warehouses. This would allow the network to maximize the utilization of their physical assets and increase revenue from underutilized assets. But they need a trust layer, an accountability layer, which is blockchain.

In March 2018 at SxSW, I met Shelita Burke who left Microsoft as a data scientist and cryptographer to become a full-time musician. As a musician and a cryptographer, she understood the power of blockchain in music rights distribution. Ms. Burke wanted to solve the issue of slow royalty payments in the industry. She created the first generation of musicians to put their music metadata in blockchain. Burke also made her music available via Bitcoin. Payments that came into the Ethereum smart contract would be automatically distributed to her collaborators in a fully transparent environment. Her story can be found here.[1]

Technically, a musician putting her royalty distribution in a smart contract is no different than a logistics company putting their shipment contract with counterparties in a smart contract. The nature of the

---

[1] E. Blake. October 20, 2017. "How Pop Artist Shelita Burke Uses Data Science and Blockchain To Her Advantage," *Forbes*.

problem may be different, but technicalities of how it is solved using blockchain may be similar.

The point here is that cross-pollination between domains about the use of blockchain in solving problems is an invaluable exercise. I learned a lot from talking to the musician, furniture retailer, transportation engineer, and many others. Most importantly, I incorporated those ideas into my own startup and shared them with individuals from other sectors.

Push Back Against Familiarity Bias

During my dozen or so workshops and webinars, I have come across individuals who think blockchain technology will have slower adoption than technologies that they are familiar with, such as automated vehicles and 3D printing. I believe this phenomenon is like familiarity bias, commonly mentioned in investor circles. Investors who are unfamiliar with a technology will underestimate it compared with the ones they are familiar with.

Individuals intimately involved with automated and connected vehicles, who are used to slower adoption of technologies, said that few companies would adopt blockchain, or that it would take a long time to reach that point. Or they question that blockchain will have widespread use in mobility. What they do not know is that open source technology such as blockchain spreads like wildfire.

Technologies such as automated vehicles are at the mercy of a handful of companies, and once they are released they will be heavily regulated by the government, primarily for reasons of public safety. Blockchain technology is not owned by anyone. There are no handful of companies that control the flow of blockchain technology adoption. Nobody owns patents or rights to it. It is largely open source, and I would argue that it has a much bigger development community than automated vehicles.

Calling Out the Saying "Blockchain Is Not Ready"

Any new technology is bound to receive backlash from doubters regarding its potential. A refrain I often hear at conferences is that blockchain, especially public blockchain, is not ready for business because (1) Bitcoin can only do *x transactions per second, or TPS,* and Ethereum is *seven TPS,* so it has a scaling problem, (2) We don't understand cryptocurrency, and (3) the price is too volatile.

I then argue that it is not blockchain that is not ready but businesses that are not ready to use blockchain. Blockchain is extremely efficient in implementing horizontal collaborative models that business entities are not used to. Businesses have long operated as silos with fully centralized data in a controlled environment. Blockchain is best utilized when sharing a ledger or being on a platform where a ledger is shared with other companies. This means revealing information as a trade-off to participate in a collaborative environment to gain new business and efficiency. If companies do not have a business reason to do so, then it is not blockchain's problem, it is a business problem.

That is one reason for calling out the negative sentiment. The second reason is simpler: Most executives do not have a well-rounded knowledge about blockchain. Hopefully, this book will help. Most executives I have talked with have conflicting information about blockchain's most efficient use cases, which then circles back to the earlier reason.

Don Quixote Problem of Finding a Problem that Fits the Solution

In July 2018, Forbes author Jose E. Campos wrote an article titled "Blockchain and the Don Quixote de La Mancha Syndrome."[2] In the article, Mr. Campos discussed the fallacy of blockchain evangelists trying to find the perfect problem for a new innovative technology the same way Don Quixote, a fictitious character from the year 1600, did.

Quixote believed that his chivalry would rid the world of wickedness ensuing his insanity and create nonexistent beliefs. Mr. Campos's argument was whether in the effort to justify blockchain we are creating nonexistent problems and blindly trying to use blockchain to solve them. On the contrary, blockchain should address new opportunities such as the

---

[2] J.E. Campos. July 26, 2018. "Blockchain and the Don Quixote de La Mancha Syndrome," *Forbes.* https://www.forbes.com/sites/forbesbooksauthors/2018/07/26/blockchain-and-the-don-quixote-de-la-mancha-syndrome/#4f1e0f5b4cd6.

ones we are aware of but that have been difficult to implement. Creating highly liquid peer-to-peer digital assets is one example.

"Do You Need Blockchain?" Is That The Right Question?

In 2017 and 2018, blockchain reached its hype, the price of crypto collapsed, reality set in among entrepreneurs and investors, and the question "do you need blockchain?" became omnipresent. There are numerous flowcharts to determine whether your solution or company needs blockchain or not.[3] News articles and blogs contended that in most cases databases are enough and asserted that you don't need consensus for everything.

The right statement is that I do not need blockchain if I want to run my business the same way I've run for the past 20 years, and, for that matter, I do not need any new emerging technology. Do I need AI, IoT, or machine learning? No.

But what if I want to transform my business in the next decade and be competitive, improving my operation significantly. Then, yes, I need to explore blockchain along with other emerging technologies.

Whether you need blockchain or not should not be argued on the basis of the technicalities of blockchain versus spreadsheet or database. The argument should center around the future-proofing of your business. It should be based on whether you want to create new business models and trump your competition.

If a company has a problem that can be solved using blockchain, most likely there are others that can be helped as well. Increasingly, consortiums have become a prevalent way for companies to educate themselves and collaborate to develop blockchain solutions. Becoming part of an alliance is an easy first step to join the blockchain bandwagon moving toward implementation.

---

[3]K. Wust and A. Gervais. August 28, 2018. "Do You Need a Blockchain?", *Proceedings of Crypto Valley Conference on Blockchain Technology.* https://eprint.iacr.org/2017/375.pdf.

CHAPTER 15

Understanding Implementation Risks Early On

Let me start by defining what I mean by implementation. For the record, it means a company successfully deploying some sort of application for end users or several companies collaborating to build a mutually beneficial consortium to pursue an idea. In both cases, public blockchain is utilized as the core ledger for transactions. Third-party applications and protocols are also utilized and built on public blockchain.

The reason early authors and evangelists of blockchain ensured that the technology stayed open source was to allow our imagination to take its course and let people create innovative applications or systems. Although it is clear from Satoshi Nakamoto's white paper and subsequent publications, blockchain was meant to create alternative systems (the same way Bitcoin created an alternate monetary system) that emphasized decentralization of the power structure that current institutions use.

Risks Associated with Public Blockchain Infrastructure

An investor in 2019, while doing due diligence, sent over a list of risks associated with using public blockchain infrastructure in the context of dexFreight, which in mid-2019 was a centralized marketplace platform leveraging public blockchain infrastructure. It was not yet the decentralized platform that we had envisioned. Some of the risks mentioned to us by the potential investors are quite silly. However, some were valid and are as follows:

- Won't public blockchain's size be a problem in terms of performance?

Blockchain capacity measured by the block heights is linear—a long chain of blocks linked together. As more and more transactions are created, the chain gets longer and the block height increases. Proof of work consensus algorithm needs to work harder. Hence, the investor thought we would be impacted by the fact that a longer blockchain means a slower blockchain. It is true from the outset, however, there are side chains and sharding techniques being developed to reduce transaction speed. On the other hand, mining hardware is becoming more and more computationally powerful, meaning hashing power has been increasing following Metcalf's law.

- Will reliance on third-party protocols create legal problems?

The use of decentralized services such as InterPlanetary File System (IPFS) and Ethereum can create problems for enterprise users in case the underlying blockchain is hacked, attacked, or double-pledged. You do not have a 1-800 number to call and complain. However, open infrastructure has an advantage over closed ones in that they tend to be patched quite quickly because there are so many users looking at the code, and the incentive to patch security holes is not concentrated on a single party. In the early days of Linux, it was extremely unstable. But it has been battle tested so much that Linux is often preferred over other operating systems for complex and sensitive back-end infrastructure.

- What happens if public blockchain goes through a hard fork and now there are two chains with the same historical transaction data?

It is true you will end up with two separate chains with the same transaction information of your customers, as Figure 15.1 shows. What is the problem here? There is duplicate data in two separate chains. Moving forward, you will have to choose which side of the fork to continue to use. That means the new data will be inside one of the forks.

- Who has the fiduciary duty if your data is corrupted?

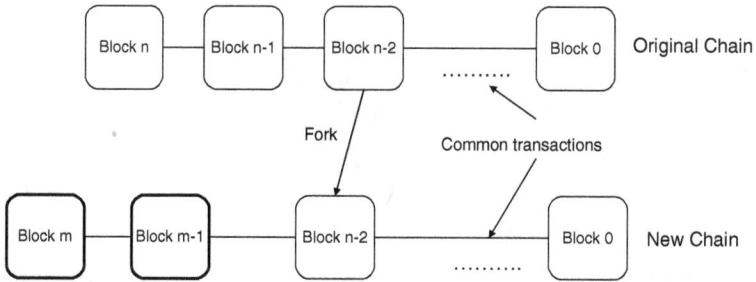

Figure 15.1 Hard fork of a blockchain that results in creation of new chain at the point of such fork

If your transactions are stored in Amazon Web Service or Azure and they are hacked with databases corrupted, the recourse is to recover the data from backups maintained by those companies. You may have to sue them to pay for the damage caused by the corruption of your data. Obviously, if it is your fault for not using strong password protection or a faulty code base, then good luck. In public blockchain, copies of transactions are stored in thousands of nodes. No, you cannot sue the Ethereum Foundation, EOS, or Bitcoin Core Developers, but your transaction data is, by design, redundant. The likelihood of data corruption is significantly low already.

- Aren't transactions in public blockchain cumbersome to audit?

In a hybrid implementation model, as described in Chapter 18, actual attributes of transactions are stored in a cloud or in-site servers. Public blockchain is used to anchor transactions and store transfer of ownership. Transaction hashes and smart contract addresses are then stored off-chain as a reference. Auditors can easily confirm transaction hashes from the user's cloud database with the ones in a public blockchain by using blockchain explorers.

- Won't the inability to move transaction history to another blockchain be a problem?

A potential investor once asked me how I would move my transaction from one blockchain to another. How do you move transactions from Ethereum to Bitcoin? The answer is "why do you need to move those transactions in the first place?" They are already recorded in Ethereum's blockchain infrastructure. The answer to that question is centered on interoperability.

Be Realistic about Transaction Speed

In conversations, executives always bring up the speed of public blockchain. Typically, the conversation starts out with, "Well, I heard Bitcoin can only do less than 10 transactions per second, so how will your solution process 100,000 daily shipments since you are built on top of Bitcoin?" Or worse, "I heard blockchain cannot scale because Bitcoin cannot process more than 10 transactions per second." In the section Side Chain and Layer 2 Solutions, I briefly talked about how the scaling of public blockchain is being resolved.

Nonetheless, let us get a few things straight. What does transaction speed mean? If it means receiving the full confirmation from the network that the transaction has been added to a block and 51 percent of miners have added the block to the blockchain, then it is true: Bitcoin cannot process more than 10 transactions per second. However, we should ask whether we have transactions that need instantaneous confirmation and entry into a ledger.

In most life use cases, the answer is "probably not." In commercial applications, entry into a ledger happens much after a transaction has been initiated. After two parties enter into an agreement, the hash of the agreement can stay in the public blockchain as an unconfirmed transaction (UTXO) until it is confirmed in the next block. Payment is an issuance that happens much after services are rendered. In the supply chain, shipments are delivered instantly, and may take several hours or days.

Finding an Internal Champion

Companies that I have worked with had one thing in common—they had an internal champion at C-Suite or VP level. They are either enthusiastic about adopting blockchain technology to ride the wave or understand that the blockchain fits naturally into their mission to increase digitization of their operations. They are the ambassadors and believers of this technology.

Almost all initial contacts were with senior executives, who then chaperoned other midlevel IT folks and business development managers into the conversation. As expected, their knowledge about blockchain was rudimentary and high-level yet strategic.

The point I am trying to make is that having an internal champion at the senior level helps move implementation much faster. However, as we often experienced, they did not have a clear requirement from individuals at the ground level who are either unable or unwilling to adopt new applications. This created a conflict between the champion and midlevel managers. Hence, at dexFreight, we always emphasize that the requirements come from the bottom and not from the top.

We also asked that companies assign a midlevel manager as a point of contact to work with us, but we kept the champion updated about the progress of implementation. For our part, we stayed cognizant of potential conflict between the internal champion and people below. We ensured that the latter are ultimately won over by demonstrating value propositions to increase their operational performance.

Stakeholder Participation

Over a period of 3 years, I have discussed the merits of using blockchain with hundreds of people from all over the world. They each have their own perspectives regarding why blockchain may or may not be valuable in their respective companies and in the domain they operate in. I shall now divide these individuals into five groups, and I'm certain these are the categories of stakeholders a company must deal with to implement blockchain:

The "Don't care" group—These stakeholders do not care about why and how blockchain is being implemented. If the application works and it does what it was intended to do, who cares what is running in the background? End users who work in the application daily typically represent this group.

"Sounds great, but" group—This group has bought into the hype, studied it, and understands the problems that lie ahead. However, this group needs more thorough vetting of return on investment (ROI). This is the most difficult group to convince. But once they are convinced, they will turn into champions of the cause.

"Let's do it because I know the blockchain" group—This group understands blockchain well. They are convinced that the project should be funded and implemented.

"I made money in Bitcoin" group—These are individuals hiding in the corporate closet. They have studied blockchain, bought crypto, made a small fortune, and will now support the project out of either genuine enthusiasm or a desire to avoid being hypocritical. Most likely you will not be able to pinpoint stakeholders in this category because they have chosen not to reveal that they've made a small fortune by buying Bitcoin early on.

Identifying Pain Points Where Blockchain Can Impact Is Critical

In my conversations with shippers and manufacturers, both small and large, they mention that their biggest pain point is waste of resources to reconcile erroneous invoices they receive from carriers and brokers, especially small ones. Even though it's not their fault, these companies must expend valuable resources to fix invoices before they issue payments to those carriers and brokers. Sometimes, carriers will complain that their payments are being deliberately delayed by the shippers while the invoices are being checked and double checked.

This is an excellent use case, or pain point, that can be solved by using smart contracts signed by both shippers and carriers. In this case, blockchain functions like an immutable contract code that nobody can unilaterally tamper with. The smart contract can then release payments to carriers as per the terms coded into the contract and agreed on by both parties. Hence, selection of use cases should be such that they involve multiple parties, preferably external entities such as subcontractors and vendors. This is a use case to align business processes vertically between entities and their contractors and vendors.

Another group of use case is where multiple parties align business processes into a horizontal platform where they collaborate to share resources, information, and decisions using blockchain as a neutral source of truth. Multiple parties collaborating on a horizontal platform are a much more compelling use case than the vertical one because companies can force their vendors and subcontractors to use the existing, centralized, nonblockchain system.

An example of collaborations among competing entities includes multiple hospitals that can collaborate to share patient information to reduce redundancies in entering insurance and patient history. In the supply chain, multiple carriers share trucks, dispatchers, and drivers in order to maintain customer satisfaction during peak seasons and in uncertain environments. Manufacturers can collaborate to reduce the cost of verifying vendors without having to run background checks and even share performance issues.

An example of the second type of horizontal collaboration includes the public and private sector entities that operate either an airport or a seaport by creating a single platform, increasing accountability and efficiency of container movement in and out of the port. In this example, entities do not have noncompeting interests.

A carrier's interest is to pick up containers from the port and deliver them on time. A customs agency's interest is to ensure contrabands and illegal goods are not exported or imported. They are also tasked to collect tariffs. A terminal operator's interest is to safely load and unload containers from ships. All these agencies operate on an equal footing yet have specific objectives.

Dealing with Identity

Bitcoin's audacity was allowing people to spend and receive bitcoins without showing any government-provided identification, in the same way that I do not need to show my driver's license to give someone a $20 bill. To spend bitcoins, all you need to do is authenticate the transaction with a private and a public key. You can generate as many private and public keys as you want to keep your assets safe.

You can give the key to anyone, causing the bitcoins associated with the key to belong to the recipient. I can give the private key to my 3-year-old niece, and all the Bitcoin associated with that key is hers. It is truly peer to peer like cash. There is no hierarchy. Everyone is treated equally. Many other cryptocurrencies work in a similar fashion.

Now, let us talk about what sort of identity would be required to transfer nonfungible, legal assets on blockchain. I am talking about physical assets such as homes, land, and cars. The problem with transferring these assets is that without a trusted third party such as the government, it is infeasible in today's economic world. Individuals must provide all types of identifiable documents to complete those asset transfers.

Disclosure of such documents is sometimes required by law to reduce risk and liability on behalf of institutions underwriting the transfer. It is obvious that some form of virtual identity, backed by what David Birch from Hyperion Consulting calls mundane, or real identity, would be needed.[1] You can have several virtual identities, just as you can create several private keys to transact on Bitcoin or Ethereum. Unless you are using centralized exchanges, you do not need "mundane" identity to create private keys for your virtual identity.

I argue that multiple virtual identities will be challenged legally when it comes to exchanging assets that are regulated by the government because it would put an undue burden on regulatory agencies to keep track of your virtual identities. It does not matter whether blockchain keeps track of transactions using those identities. On the flip side, Mr. Birch's prediction may come true in that regulated institutions may play a role in managing our virtual identities while real identities would be a personal black box secured with individuals. I am excited about the prospects of this happening.

Let us change course a bit. Individuals can create multiple virtual identities from their real identity to transfer assets, and blockchain would maintain an immutable ledger of those transactions occurring using virtual identities.

Still, how do we deal with organizations and legal entities exchanging nonfungible assets? What would identity management look like in organizations for its employees to interact with decentralized applications or platforms? The problem is hierarchy in organizations.

Rana Basu, a cofounder of Consurgo and Ondiflo, reminds me of it every time we talk. Mr. Basu says, yes, there are flatter organizations, but hierarchies exist—supervisors, managers, directors, vice presidents, and so on. Identity of the organization itself is created by the legal jurisdiction it is in.

For employees who work for the organization, identity is provided by the organization. They cannot create it unilaterally. An employee's identity can be revoked or can expire. They cannot keep it after leaving

---

[1]D. Birch. 2016. "How to Use Identity and Blockchain," Dutch Blockchain Conference. https://www.youtube.com/watch?v=hS15p5V3slg.

the organization. Identity is also associated with job responsibility, which follows the organization hierarchy. If they are to interact with dApps or platforms that use smart contracts, then they need to create private/public keys. They must be associated with their employee identification, which brings up the need for internal key management, policies, and procedures.

What happens to those keys if they leave the job? A company-provided employee identification can be easily deprecated, but private keys are globally unique and stay within public blockchain transactions.

Let's imagine you are building an application/platform for your customers. The product includes users who interact with smart contracts in public blockchain. There are two user requirements with regard to identity verification—a simple verification of a user's e-mail and the one in which the user is required to present a form of government-issued identification. For a product that requires simple e-mail verification, private/public key management can be self-sovereign or use third-party, decentralized solutions such as SHO Card and CIVIC.

For a product that requires the second verification type, onboarding users require KYC. It includes verification of government-provided authority to operate and function in their legal jurisdictions. A company's existence as an entity is one thing, but they may have operating authorities with time as well as other conditional limits. Their authority may be revoked owing to violations, which adds complexity to the key management issues.

CHAPTER 16

The Gold Rush of Blockchain Standards

A sharp increase has occurred with regard to the "We need blockchain standards" cry.[1] To most blockchain observers, and even for practitioners like myself, it is difficult to grasp what blockchain standards entail. What does it even mean? What part of blockchain are we standardizing, and, most, importantly, why? People who argue for blockchain standards point to many other standards, such as Internet Protocol, HTTP, Wi-Fi, and Bluetooth. Their argument is that blockchain will achieve the same level of adoption as hardware devices and web applications that we have experienced because of these other standards.

Perhaps that is true. Perhaps it is not the right time. Perhaps standards at this time will stifle the competition and consolidate the market in the hands of a few corporations. Some have even elevated the concern to the extent that the technology will not survive without standards. Nonetheless, these questions are difficult to answer. What we are left with now is pure speculation. Moody has reported that blockchain technology will break the chasm and experience wider adoption in 2021.[2] One of the reasons for such a breakthrough is standardization, which will promote asset securitization.

---

[1]L. Yaffe. March 30, 2018. "Blockchain — We Need Standardization," *Medium Corporation*. https://medium.com/@lyaffe/blockchain-we-need-standardization-68b358f42daf.

[2]T. Abrosimova. September 9, 2019. "Blockchain Technology to Have Standards by 2021- Moody's," *FXStreet*. https://www.fxstreet.com/cryptocurrencies/news/blockchain-technology-to-have-standards-by-2021-moodys-201909091032.

At present, blockchain technology is fragmented with many incompatible protocols. This fragmentation raises concerns about interoperability between different flavors of blockchain. If there is one reason to call for standardization, then in my opinion it is interoperability. If we do not solve the issue of interoperability, new business models will require a middle layer that works like a bridge between multiple flavors of blockchain. These bridges will become a vulnerable third party if not decentralized from the get-go.

Timing is a somewhat debated topic. I say "somewhat" because I see more opinions favoring "we have to do it now whether we like it or not." A Finextra blog post in 2018/2019 argued that we ought to wait because most blockchain platforms are not "mature enough to have their developers and backers discuss ledger *interoperability* productively." If the emphasis is on interoperability, then it is the elephant in the room and must be solved within the next few years. However, history tells us that interoperability has not stopped us from innovating and creating new business models.

Dozens of different flavors of blockchain exist, and new ones will keep popping up every year. If we are to wait for most blockchains to mature, then it will be a long time before we even start building standards. Two public blockchains with the highest market capitalization, Bitcoin and Ethereum, are already being utilized to build new business models for a new economy. The argument for "let us wait" doesn't stand anymore.

Going forward, blockchain applications will need to be compliant with blockchain standards. The standards, in turn, enable the creation of tools that can be certified as being compliant. Additionally, it allows the platforms to attain a level of robustness required by enterprises.

Standardizing Blockchain Data Elements

A common legal document that companies in the logistics industry produce and widely utilize is called "bill of lading." The document is proof that a trucking company moving a shipment has been given the proper authority to do so. There is no standardized format for the bill of lading. They look similar from one company to another because they include most common and critical pieces of information such as address, shipment type, weight, classification, and price.

The bill of lading represents proof of pickup and a digital signature from the consignee as well as a geo-location that represents proof of delivery. Both data points are important in a shipment's smart contract that shipper and trucking company will digitally sign. Unless every shipper and trucking company in the world uses the same application, both shippers and trucking companies will be left with hundreds of variations of smart contracts. This would make interoperability between shippers and trucking companies' systems a nightmare.

Another example is an experience that we at the dexFreight marketplace are facing. The marketplace, unfortunately, needs to connect with multiple fleet management systems to receive telematics information of truck's locations. Trucking companies use fleet management systems (FMS) and electronic logging devices. Although their performance requirements are well defined, their data definitions are not standardized. That means, for every type of FMS that trucking companies use, we must create a "translator" to internally standardize data to send things like proof of pickup and proof of delivery to smart contracts. This puts a massive burden on us to build translators.

Instead, as Figure 16.1 shows, if FMS companies agree to adhere to Blockchain in Transport Alliance (BITA) location standards and provide an option to send location data to external entities like dexFreight, then we do not need to build those translators.

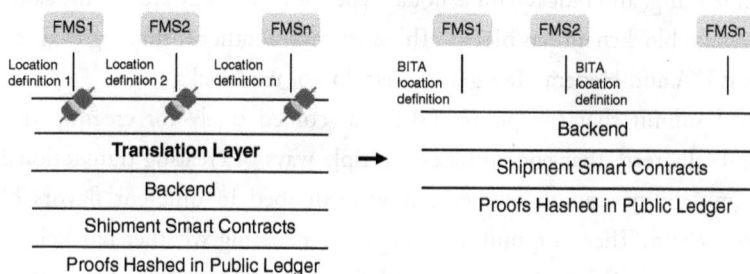

Figure 16.1 Use of location standards reduces the need for translation layer

Just from the one preceding example, there is a strong incentive for coding existing legal documents, in a standardized way, into smart contracts to minimize the need for "adapters or bridges" between different flavors of smart contracts and blockchains. Interoperability allows blockchain systems to read each other's transactions and even share digital assets stored in smart contracts of different blockchains. Hence, standardizing data used as variables in smart contracts is the first step toward achieving interoperability. However, doing so requires domain knowledge and cannot be left solely to blockchain developers.

Industry Requirements from Blockchain Standards

I am in no way involved in developing blockchain standards. On the basis of discussions online and during conferences, it appears that building "blockchain standards" is nontrivial and complex and will take years to complete.

When it comes to standards, people mention that they need a standardized definition of blockchain. To me, the definition of blockchain is simple—transactions are stored together in blocks, and blocks are chained together using cryptography. It is tamperproof and immutable using a decentralized consensus and network of nodes.

A phrase you will see quite often in publications is "Blockchain/DLT," meaning they are one and the same. In other publications, you will see blockchain mentioned as a *type* of DLT. I have received suggestions and corrections from a few that instead of the word blockchain I should use DLT so as not to limit the choice of technological terminology. Let me make my position clear on this topic. Blockchain and DLT are not the same thing, and blockchain is not a "type" of DLT. They are not the same because blockchain has blocks. There are several other technologies, such as IOTA and Hedera Hashgraph, that do not use blocks.

I submit that the phrase DLT was coined solely for creating this umbrella term that encompasses multiple ways of creating transactional immutability, and these methods were dubbed in different flavors of blockchain. There are multiple blog posts debating whether blockchain is a type of DLT or not. I do not believe that debate has been settled. Until then, like Matthew Beedham, I will take the position that blockchain and DLT are not interchangeable.[3] Although I have nothing against

---

[3]M. Beedham. July 27, 2018. "Here's the Difference between Blockchain and Distributed Ledger Technology," *TNW*. https://thenextweb.com/hardfork/2018/07/27/distributed-ledger-technology-blockchain/.

other technologies, because they have incredible potential, I refuse to mix blockchain and DLT together.

Nonetheless, as a would-be consumer of standards with the ability to speak for other companies leveraging blockchain technology, I need the following elements in place for adopting a standard or a combination of standards—(1) standardized data/parameters that are input to blockchain, likely domain specific, (2) reference architectures and implementations, again domain specific, (3) standardization of enabling components, and (4) minimum/baseline requirements for domain-specific applications such as IEEE/P2140.1—The Standard for General Requirements for Cryptocurrency Exchanges.

Standardization of data going in and out of public blockchain (domain specific)—The logistics industry has several types of nonstandardized transactions and supporting documents, such as the bill of lading, invoices, carrier-shipper agreements, and insurance if they are not using electronic data interchange (EDI). Companies have their own versions and customized attributes that they use while producing these documents. In the context of creating smart contracts in lieu of bipartite or tripartite agreements and contracts, standardization means defining a minimum set of variables in and out of smart contracts followed by standardized definitions of input and output variables. Arguably, this is highly domain- and use-case specific.

BITA is building standard definitions of many input variables for the logistics industry. Standardizing data definitions is the most difficult thing to do because it is highly granular and fundamental. On top of that, traditional industries that have existed for decades may already have data definitions that are widely used. This means standards organizations should expect pushbacks from the industry to limit variations in such definitions.

Standardization of enabling components—Core components of business applications may include smart contracts, oracles, and identity along with traditional components such as cloud services, sensors, and so forth. Standardization of these components means outlining general requirements of what kind of components are essential to a use case, how they perform in the context of those use cases, and how they interact with other components.

Baseline requirements—High-level and low-level requirements of the overall system for domain-specific use cases form a basis for reference implementations for the use case. These requirements delineate reference implementations into modules.

Reference implementations—Reference implementation simply means sample or example implementations based on which others can design and deploy future applications. Because reference implementations are purposely designed to guide future developments, they are typically put forth by standards bodies and deliberately show the use of standards (proposed or existing). Standards organizations should suggest reference implementations for use cases in different domains. Such implementations should include minimum or baseline requirements (both high and low levels), how enabling components interact, and minimum input and output data. This is like putting together previously discussed elements for specific use cases. The World Economic Forum (WEF) tool kits for supply chain are a great reference to build reference implementations. Companies desiring to build use cases for customers can then mimic the reference implementation that significantly reduces the overall design cost.

Standards Should Not Conflict

At least six different groups exist that are building blockchain standards. The one that I closely watch is the BITA because they are building standards for the logistics industry. All these standards are at early stages of development. The International Standards Organization (ISO) has announced that its standards will be ready in 2021. Because they are at early stages, it is difficult to analyze the scope of their development with regard to how I, as an application, can adopt a standard and whether I must adopt more than one. I also do not know the extent to which these standards bodies interact with each other so that there are little or no duplicate requirements.

Although you may be developing an enterprise application for a specific sector, there will be components in the application that need to follow standards designed for other sectors. For example, a logistics application may follow BITA's standards for locations and bill of lading but may need to follow pharmaceutical standards, accounting standards, and so on.

The following are the organizations building blockchain standards that I am aware of. Full disclosure: except for BITA, I know little of what their standards encompass. I strongly recommend that you monitor these standards because they publish their draft versions.

Institute of Electrical and Electronics Engineers (IEEE) DLT/blockchain standards: The IEEE is developing the IEEE P2418 series, which is focused on the creation of generic frameworks, architectures, and interoperability enabling-technology building blocks along with vertical-industry standards.

ISO/TC 307 Blockchain and DLT: TC 307 is one of the most active global standards efforts driven by the Australian standards body and the ISO. TC 307 is in the early stages for ISO 307. Several focus areas exist here, including architecture and taxonomy, security and privacy, identity, smart contracts, governance, and interoperability between blockchain applications.

Blockchain in Transport Alliance (BITA): The BITA is a membership-based alliance of companies engaged in logistics and supply chain. Their goal is to drive adoption of blockchain in the industry. One of the mandates of BITA is to develop data and information exchange standards for blockchain applications/solutions.

Mobility Open Blockchain Initiative (MOBI): The MOBI is also a membership-based alliance of auto manufacturers, parts suppliers, consulting firms, and technology providers engaged in developing standards, and other building blocks for the industry to leverage blockchain technology and build innovative mobility applications.

Enterprise Ethereum Alliance (EEA): The EEA is one of the most active industry alliances with more than 500 members working on open, standards-based architectures and specifications to accelerate the adoption of Enterprise Ethereum. They are also focusing on the development of technical specifications and certification of Ethereum for enterprise.

International Telecommunication Union-Telecommunication (ITU-T): The ITU-T has created an open-participation ITU-T FG DLT to analyze the standardization demands of applications and services built on DLT.

World Wide Web Consortium (W3C): The W3C has a blockchain community group working on a web ledger protocol to generate message format standards for blockchain based on ISO 20022, producing guidelines for the use of storage, including torrent, public blockchain, private blockchain, and sidechain. This group will study and evaluate new technologies related to blockchain and such use cases as interbank communications.

World Economic Forum (WEF): Although not a standards organization, WEF has published a series of tool kits for practitioners in the field of supply chain. Disclosure: I am a contributor in few of those tool kits.

Will Blockchain Compete with EDI Standards?

This section may seem out of place, but it will be clear in a moment why it is here. Tip: We can learn a few valuable things from EDI standards and how it became ubiquitous. EDI was first invented in the 1970s as a means by which two varying enterprise systems exchange data packets that describe documents such as invoices, order, loans, health records, and receipts in a standardized format such that both systems can easily translate the packets and recreate them as documents at the receiving system. EDI provides a technical basis for automated commercial "conversations" between two entities, either internal or external.[4]

Several EDI standards exist such as generic, and specific applications such as supply chain and healthcare. EDI as a standard is so ubiquitous that there are very few industrial sectors that do not use it. The market size of the EDI software industry is expected to reach $6 billion in 2025.[5] Millions of companies around the world use and rely on EDI to exchange information with one another. The quantitative benefit it creates for companies in terms of savings from not having to use paper or electronic documents with translations could be several hundred billion. Perhaps that is why EDI as a standard has withstood changes and disruptions in electronic communication, including the Internet. It has evolved over the years to include advances such as cryptographic and encryption techniques to secure transactions.

---

[4]"Electronic Data Interchange," *Wikipedia.* https://en.wikipedia.org/wiki/Electronic_data_interchange, (accessed November 20, 2019).

[5]M. Bryant. September 6, 2017. "EDI Market Growing at 9.4% CAGR, Could Near $6B by 2025," *HealthCareDrive.* https://www.healthcaredive.com/news/edi-market-growing-at-94-cagr-could-near-6b-by-2025/504282/.

When I first started evangelizing blockchain to logistics and transportation industries, I was constantly asked, "Will blockchain replace EDI and make it obsolete?" The logistics sector is one of the largest users of EDI, accounting for the curiosity among executives. My answer was and still is a resounding *no*, at least not in the foreseeable future. Here are the top reasons why:

- Business reason—millions of companies use EDI every second (many of them do not even know they are using EDI), and an entire industry exists to support EDI translation, maintenance, and integration. Companies have spent billions over the last three decades implementing systems that use EDI standards. It is unlikely that they will abandon EDI anytime soon.
- Technical reason—EDI is a data formatting standard for transactions. In its primitive state, blockchain is a ledger of transactions. The former defines how a data packet being transmitted should appear. The latter creates a digital fingerprint of data being transmitted and records it in an immutable ledger.

Instead, EDI will benefit from blockchain technology, ensuring that the EDI data being transmitted has not been tampered with by comparing a unique hash (of EDI data) before and after transmission. This is to confirm proof of integrity and proof of transmission between two systems belonging to two different entities, eliminating the need for EDI systems to acknowledge the transmission of data and, instead, receive proof of transmission from the blockchain.[6] I imagine two systems not requiring each other to verify data transmission using EDI and instead using public blockchain, saving considerable time and money. Another significant value proposition is that both systems can independently verify proof of transmission and integrity.

In the example shown in Figure 16.2, Company A will convert its invoice into relevant standards format using an EDI translator and transmit

---

[6]M. Wallgren. March 26, 2018. "EDI and Blockchain - A Match Made in Heaven?", *LinkedIn*. https://www.linkedin.com/pulse/edi-blockchain-match-made-heaven-mathias-wallgren/.

the data packet to a vendor or a customer, which does the same to reconcile the invoice and issue payment.

However, in the preceding example, Company A does not know that the EDI translator sent the correct PO data in EDI format to Company B and C, even though Company A may get a copy of the EDI data sent. Hence, Company A must "trust" the EDI translator. Company B and C then go ahead and fulfill the PO, sending the invoice back to A via the EDI translator. I would imagine that fraud could occur. However, the back office must verify the documents to prevent such a possibility.

EDI is designed to operate in a one-way, two-party data communication. If the communication involves a third party, then it is left out of the communication. Instead, it must receive a replica of the data packet from one or both parties. Using blockchain, as Figure 16.3 shows, hash or digital signature of the EDI data packet is added to blockchain along with the public key of the sender. All three parties shown in the example can confirm that they have, in fact, received untampered information, which will reduce the probability of disputes.[7]

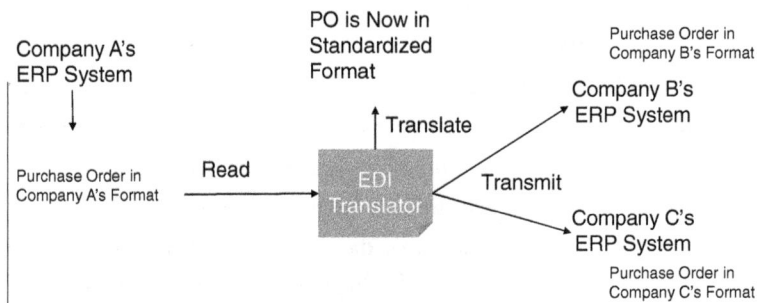

Figure 16.2 Current process of translating invoices using the EDI

This might be a primary advantage of blockchain in today's EDI world, the ability to proactively resolve disputes between businesses by allowing parties to continuously monitor the blockchain for any disparities

---

[7]S.S. Naruka and R. Rengamannar. August 2019. "Improved EDI with Blockchain," *Wipro Limited*. https://www.wipro.com/en-US/blogs/surendra-singh-naruka/improvededi-visibility-with-blockchain/.

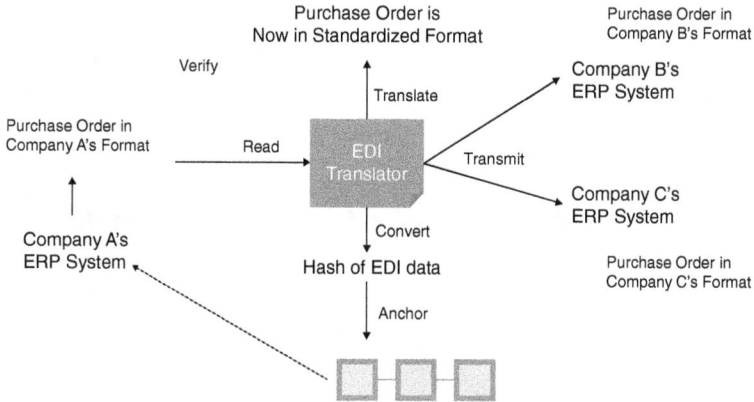

Figure 16.3 Use of blockchain to anchor EDI data for verification process

in the transaction, something EDI does not provide.[8] Perhaps in the future, instead of companies sending data wrapped in EDI standards to each other, they can simply add the transaction to the blockchain and provide each other with the proof of transaction, as well as the keys to view details of the transaction.

EDI standardization took years to complete because it was purposed to be sector agnostic, encompassing hundreds of different document types such as purchase orders, bills of lading, and invoices. Developing blockchain standards will take years because people are building applications in every sector imaginable. There will be demands to "translate" traditional documents to add to blockchain. For example, how should one put invoice information into public or private blockchain? How should someone maintain privacy? How can one make it flexible enough for parties to obfuscate sensitive information? At present, companies that provide EDI translation middle layers have access to their customers' information being translated and moved back and forth. Will the blockchain community accept such a middle translation layer however decentralized it may be?

---

[8]M. Kersels. October 28, 2019. "Part 1: EDI – The Platypus of B2B?", *SAP Community*. https://blogs.sap.com/2019/10/04/part-1-edi-the-platypus-of-b2b/.

CHAPTER 17

Engaging in Blockchain Implementation

Implementation does not mean turning your existing company into a decentralized entity or a decentralized autonomous organization (DAO), the result of a long and hard inward decision among the company's stakeholders. In this chapter, I simply advocate that companies dabble in public blockchain by "trying" different methods to participate in decentralized economy, the Web 3 movement, and, most importantly, utilizing public blockchain infrastructure in their product offering. For companies, none of this is easy because there are risks associated with doing so, such as wasting resources, credibility, and even time. Hence, it is prudent to perform due diligence and risk analysis before engaging with startups or using decentralized services.

A culmination of these activities described in what follows is what companies and I hope will maximize utilization of public blockchain infrastructure in their product offering to customers. Companies can engage in the following activities simultaneously or concurrently depending on the availability of internal resources for participation and a keen interest among the management.

Joining the Web 3.0 Movement

John Markoff, of the *New York Times,* described Web 3.0 in his 2006 article, "Entrepreneurs See a Web Guided by Common Sense," as the next stage in the evolution of the Internet, which would be more of a guide than a catalog of information,[1] an Internet that can reason in a human

---

[1] J. Markoff. November 12, 2006. "Entrepreneurs See a Web Guided by Common Sense," *The New York Times.* https://www.nytimes.com/2006/11/12/business/12web.html.

fashion. Mr. Markoff wrote, "…a system that can give a reasonable and complete response to a simple question like, 'I am looking for a warm place to vacation and I have a budget of $ 3,000.00. Oh, and I have an 11-year-old child.'" In today's system, such a query can lead to hours of sifting through lists of flights, hotel, and car rentals. The options are often at odds with one another. Under Web 3.0, the same search would ideally turn up a complete vacation package that was planned as meticulously as if it had been assembled by a human travel agent—in short, an Internet that can not only list things collected from a vast web of databases, but also perform intelligent tasks. Perhaps Web 3.0 = current Internet + AI?

Fast forward to 2014, crypto and blockchain enthusiasts started talking about Web 3.0 as a decentralized web, the way it was meant to be before big corporations took over and consolidated information in servers. I don't know when and how the definition of Web 3.0 changed from semantic web to decentralized web. I suppose it does not matter.

Jutta Steiner, CEO and cofounder of Parity Technologies, described in a blog post, "What the heck is Web 3.0 anyway?", Web 3.0 as a new wave of networking technologies that promise to return the Internet to the hands of users.[2] Ms. Steiner called it a movement that utilizes advances in peer-to-peer technology such as blockchain to build services that prioritizes the protection of users over profiting. Mr. Matteo Zago, cofounder of Essentia.one, called it a "pro-privacy and anti-monopoly" web and the antithesis of companies such as Facebook and Uber.[3]

It is important to understand that whatever the scope of Web 3.0, semantic, decentralized web, or both, its purpose is to restructure the way in which the Internet is accessed and interacted with.[4] Web 3.0 is

---

[2]J. Steiner. October 26, 2018. "What the Heck is Web 3.0 Anyway?", *Forbes*. https://www.forbes.com/sites/juttasteiner/2018/10/26/what-the-heck-is-web-3-0-anyway/#725ffea66614.

[3]M. Zago. January 30, 2018. "Why the Web 3.0 Matters and You Should Know About It," *Medium Corporation*. https://medium.com/@matteozago/why-the-web-3-0-matters-and-you-should-know-about-it-a5851d63c949.

[4]Bitfish. December 6, 2018. "The Decentralized Internet is Here: Web 3.0 and the Future of Blockchain-Powered Future," *Medium Corporation*. https://medium.com/bitfishlabs/the-decentralized-internet-is-here-web-3-0-and-the-future-of-blockchain-powered-future-f16ff02584a9.

the decentralized web in which information stays within the firewall of the users and inside of their nodes, mobile phones, and browsers. Their data is not "rented" out by big corporations without fair compensation to individual users and without opting in to do so.

In Web 3.0, the users decide what data to share and with whom. This is a use case of the decentralized web I am excited about—bringing computing where the data resides and transferring value to other users. In the section "Tokenized Data Sharing," I talk about how tokens will be used in the peer-to-peer world to "lease" data without facilitation by intermediaries.

Web 3.0 is widely believed to be the next stage of the evolution of Web 2.0, in which data stays with users. It would take a nostalgic turn to the vision of the Web 2.0 and will be the antithesis of today's platforms. Platform owners will have to rent data from users rather than the other way around. Instead of data leaving a user's machine and going to platform owners, computation will be performed at the owner's machine and the result then sent back to the platform.

This paradigm shift changes the way the Internet transfers value among users and creates new opportunities not monopolized by big corporations or governments. The Internet was designed to be stateless to enable it to function with high speed. With Web 1.0, servers merely routed data to one another. Web 2.0 evolved into big corporations storing state information and creating value for themselves by selling data for advertisement revenue.[5]

On the other hand, individual users have no efficient way to transfer their state, for instance, by leasing their browsing history and monetizing it. In the decentralized web, businesses can "lease" their data and monetize it, whereas they have no way to do that now. In Web 3.0, public blockchain is that missing "state layer" that is available to everybody in a permissionless network.

A decentralized web with distributed applications will allow businesses to keep the data behind a "firewall," and the marketplace will aggregate

---

[5]E. Tekisalp. August 29, 2018. "Understanding Web 3 — A User Controlled Internet," *Coinbase Blog.* https://blog.coinbase.com/understanding-web-3-a-user-controlled-internet-a39c21cf83f3.

data from multiple businesses, paying royalty to them via smart contracts and blockchain storing provenance of data between users without big corporations as intermediaries.

The reality is that incumbent companies cannot decentralize their user data so easily. That may require a complete pivot of the company's operating model and threaten the company's existence. Instead, these companies can become a contributor to a public utility DAO or participate in blockchain/smart contract-enabled Web 3 data marketplaces.

Monetizing and Sharing Data in Marketplaces

Blockchain provides a neutral, trusted layer for companies to exchange data and ensure anonymity. This allows stakeholders in a consortium to contribute to data pools without the other party knowing which stakeholder added the data. They will only know that one of the stakeholders did indeed contribute data. As the number of stakeholders grow, the value of a data pool increases and provides stakeholders access to richer data they didn't have before.

A simple use case is private companies sharing data with government entities for threat intelligence and policy planning. I've described further on a use case, although hypothetical, in which trucking companies and shippers share operational information with state and federal government for the latter to use the data for purposes that include infrastructure improvement and freight corridor planning. In this example, companies will share origin destination, shipment type, and price information with the government.

Obviously, legal and contractual instruments should be in place for this kind of data sharing mechanism to occur. There should be proper incentives or rewards for companies to contribute data. With the ledger existing outside of the federal systems, and digital hash of information submitted to the ledger, motor carriers can rest assured that their information has not been tampered with or altered in any way.

The neutral data exchange platform can be built on top of the underlying blockchain protocol, whether public or private. The platform includes a user interface to interact with the blockchain. The blockchain stores digital fingerprints, or hashes of data, submitted by state agencies and trucking companies.

As Figure 17.1 shows, a trucking company publishes metadata to the platform, which then sends a hash value of the metadata to blockchain. The platform then makes the metadata available for the government to view and download the data. Governments can verify whether the data has not been tampered with by comparing the hash of metadata they received with the hash value in the blockchain. If both hashes are equal, that means the data has not been tampered with. Smart contracts will enforce payment or reward (if available) to the trucking company and reveal encryption keys if required by the trucking company. I published a blog post describing a similar concept to create a Web 3.0 logistics data marketplace.

The benefit of this kind of arrangement is that the data can stay within the trucking company's firewall while a smart contract is used as a mechanism to enforce payment to the trucking companies. Data from multiple trucking companies can be pooled. Proportionate rewards to trucking companies are then encoded in the smart contract.

Companies will have to make a policy decision about whether to participate in the marketplace or not and which attributes of data should be published in the marketplace. Also, it might be better for companies to participate in a data pool rather than publish data individually such that the company's data is mingled with data from other companies. Decisions to participate in data marketplaces should not be taken lightly, because competitors may gain unwanted knowledge of a company's operations.

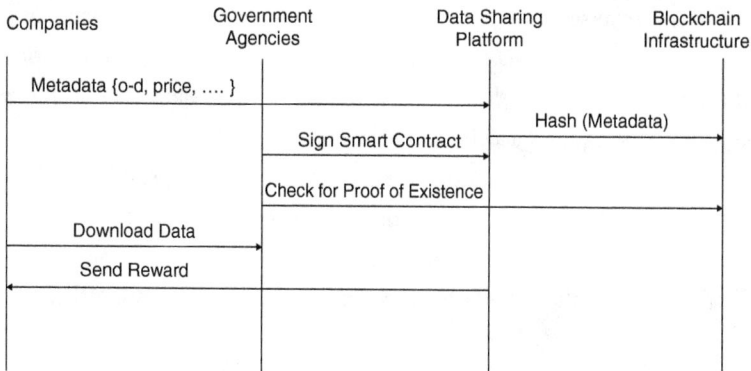

Figure 17.1 Secure and trusted data exchange between private and government entities using blockchain as a trusted infrastructure

Participating in Consortia and Alliances

I have not found consistent distinctions between consortia and alliances. They are often used interchangeably. For the sake of simplicity, I'll define alliances as membership-driven organizations that are not picky about who joins them if they operate within the industry that the alliance caters to. Examples are the Blockchain in Transport Alliance (BITA) and the Mobility Open Blockchain Initiative (MOBI). Their objectives are diverse, including creating blockchain-related standards, educating members, and performing proof of concepts.

Alliances may be domain specific. BITA caters to logistics companies and solution providers. MOBI caters to auto manufacturers. Members pay annual dues, which are used to perform tasks outlined by the alliance. The Ethereum Enterprise Alliance has diverse membership and caters to companies in a large spectrum of industries. The Blockchain Interoperability Alliance, R3, and Trusted IoT Alliances are subject to focused alliances.

On the other hand, consortia are industry focused, with a limited number of tightly knit companies. They may not be membership driven but have "banded together" to perform a specific set of objectives. Most often, they have a small number of participants and pool funds to perform a proof of concept and pilot projects. Consortia are effective in pursuing proof of concepts because of their size.

There are many reasons why companies join, and ought to join, consortia and alliances. Deloitte, in 2019, interviewed about 1400 companies and found diverse expectations for joining consortia. Such expectations included cost savings, accelerated learning, risk sharing, building critical adoption, maintaining relevance, and influencing standards,[6] the top two being cost savings and accelerated learning.

The result is the formation of regional ad hoc groups, cooperatives, and regional alliances. Most of them are industry agnostic and aim to increase the adoption of blockchain in their regions. The Austin Blockchain Cooperative and the Florida Blockchain Foundation are among them.

---

[6]"Deloitte's 2019 Global Blockchain Survey," *Deloitte Development LLC*, https://www2.deloitte.com/content/dam/Deloitte/se/Documents/risk/DI_2019-global-blockchain-survey.pdf, (accessed December 28, 2019).

Joining alliances is an easy path to get on the blockchain "co-petition." It can be an effective platform to share ideas, lessons learned from internal pilots, and education. Sometimes I fail to see how alliances with hundreds and thousands of members benefit their members, especially small ones, except by way of getting discounts to attend conferences.

I have been critical of alliances and have refused to join some unless I have a voice in the discussion. Without pointing fingers at any alliances, I merely note that some of them prefer (without mentioning explicitly) not to engage small members, especially startups. I have also seen some companies use their membership as nothing more than a marketing gimmick. For these companies, traction from marketing is enough to justify membership.

Although I have no doubt that these alliances were formed with the best of intentions, I would advocate that you merely ensure you are part of the discussion and have opportunities to table concerns and share ideas. Otherwise, you are better off joining a mailing list and avoiding paying hefty membership dues.

Prerequisites for Implementing Blockchain Projects

When implementing a blockchain project such as a pilot or proof of concept, we must ensure that the entire predevelopment process includes clearly understood primitives (or logical components) of the system being designed. In a recent project, we proposed the following, which can be used as a template:

Data Requirements: Depending on the project, determining data requirements includes minimum attributes, velocity, latency, along with security requirements for transmission and storage. Blockchain technology is appropriate to "secure" high-frequency and low-latency data transmission because the intent of the technology is to maintain a ledger of transaction finality. Public blockchain protocols do not have enough space to store data but rather a digital fingerprint, or hash, of data and record finality between the two parties.

Data Governance: A clear governance protocol that is agreeable to all stakeholders involved in the project. Governance includes consistent methods of valuing data, pricing mechanisms, data security and audits, security of smart contracts, blockchain ledger usage to store transaction information, and data retrieval methods. An independent review board may be necessary to oversee how the underlying data is being used and consumed by the parties.

Financial Incentives: A value proposition for stakeholders involved may include financial incentives for participation. Payouts or transaction costs to be paid by the stakeholders should be clearly laid out and encoded in the smart contract(s).

Data Valuation: If the project includes monetizing data, there are no authoritative models to value the data. Consider using production and reproduction cost to value the data instead of supply-demand drive value. The second issue is that the data must be valued consistently across similar attributes, age, and geographic regions.

Confidentiality: Obfuscating human readable attributes of transactions and any other identifying information may be necessary, especially if permissionless blockchain is being considered for the project. Businesses are sensitive about not releasing their data in a public domain.

Self-Enforcing Contracts: Smart contracts perform two valuable functions—(1) automatically triggering payment to the stakeholders, and (2) removing the need to sign electronic contracts every time information is shared. The second function reduces the need to wait for invoices before issuing payments because smart contracts are presigned and agreed upon by parties who can view in the public ledger that a transaction (data transfer) has taken place.

Performing Proof of Concepts

Proof of concept (POC) is a process by which a certain idea or technology is tested for feasibility for future implementation. POCs have limited scope and focus more on technical feasibility but may also cover institutional feasibility for longer term deployment. In the blockchain world, conducting POC at enterprises and within alliances has become the norm. Implementing a nascent technology like blockchain at enterprises without proper due diligence is a risk. Hence, undertaking POCs is a hedge against institutional risks prior to future implementation, as Figure 17.2 shows.

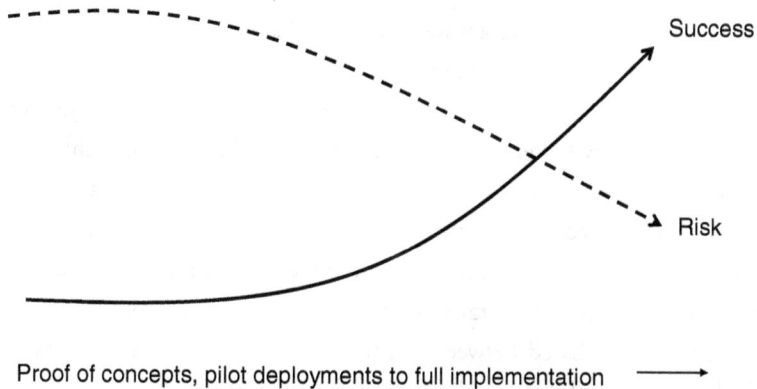

Proof of concepts, pilot deployments to full implementation ⟶

Figure 17.2 Proof of concepts and pilots reduce risk and increase success during full implementation

During POCs, exploring four key items at a high level is critical for success leading to full-scale deployment:

Clarity of benefits, challenges, and opportunities—begin by clearly identifying problems through a series of workshops and roundtables. Make sure that the right group of stakeholders is involved in the discussions. At this point, the question stakeholders should be asking is "which problems can be eliminated or alleviated by using blockchain?" Blockchain 101 for stakeholders is always a great way to start the workshop, followed by a series of intense discussions about the problems involved. In most cases, stakeholders can put two and two together to paint a clear picture of problems that can be solved by blockchain.

Discussions need to happen at multiple levels of entities involved, from c-suite to midlevel management. This avoids hiccups and roadblocks within stakeholder agencies. This series of intensive workshops should also be used to formulate high-level designs, specific requirements, and governance of the system.

Integration with legacy systems—many IT and operations managers feel that they've been blindsided by blockchain technology and that it is moving past them too rapidly. In very few instances, decisions to implement blockchain technology move bottom up. So when managers are brought into the design decisions, their instinct kicks in. Will this new system replace the one already in place? Will it impact my job? Will I have to alter the back end? When we did a POC at Port of Veracruz, initial conversations with managers were awkward because, as I could tell, they were thinking about these questions.

And then those questions slowly came out. One of the best answers to give this nervous group of managers is that blockchain technology is about creating a new ledger, which is not a new database and most likely won't replace the existing database or back end. Blockchain and the underlying ledger should not be a replacement of highly scalable and high-velocity centralized transactional databases. On the contrary, a distributed ledger shared between multiple, untrusting agencies should be deployed separately from individual agency back ends.

Success stories of blockchain applications are not well documented in the public domain. If a company or a consortium is working on a project, it hesitates to publish success stories before going into full implementation because success during a POC does not naturally translate into full implementation.

Creating a plan for a blockchain proof of concept is like any other type of project. In fact, I strongly recommend using current best practices of programming a POC added with tasks needed to understand the benefits and impact of blockchain components in the POC.

In a recent project and several proposals, I have been watching the following programming structure. The following task list was designed to build a neutral platform for a consortium of companies and agencies to collaborate more effectively and efficiently. It assumes that the agencies do not have a system that they jointly operate on and are somewhat siloed. Obviously, you will have to adjust descriptions, schedules, and other resources necessary for your POC.

Not all POCs are equally and similarly scoped. Some may simply require connecting an existing infrastructure to a public blockchain and demonstrating the benefits of smart contracts. Remember that POCs will deal not only with the technology, but also with institutional issues of putting a new system in place. In my case, this project ultimately turned into Stage 1 of the larger port community system. Hence, the scope is more comprehensive than that of a typical POC. If that is not the case for you, then the scope can be condensed into demonstrating how the technology works.

If the scope of the POC is simply to demonstrate how blockchain technology works and how it can be integrated with the existing system, then you have a much easier task in hand, because the POC can be focused to understand the benefits of using blockchain.

On the other hand, if the POC turns into a Stage 1, as in my case, then the project needs to show benefits from the system itself in addition to blockchain. The benefits of blockchain can become diluted with benefits of other technology components in the system.

Anchoring Transactions to Public Blockchain

Anchoring transactions means storing a digital fingerprint, or hash, of transactions in public blockchain as a proof of existence, as well as integrity for audits and revisions later against insurance claims, fraud, and even settling payments between parties to the transaction.

Adding transactions in public blockchain costs money, and hence you need to make a business decision about whether to anchor individual transactions or group multiple transactions into a single transaction. That business decision may be the result of providing accessibility to those transactions to users. Transactions may involve a unique set of parties. If all you need to do is provide proof of existence of a transaction, then a hash can be created of multiple transactions and added to the blockchain, as shown below. For more information, please refer to the section about how Merkle root works to determine whether a transaction exists or not.

There are two ways to anchor a transaction(s) into a public blockchain: The first method is to create a text file with transaction(s) information and use services such as Tierion to store a hash of the text file in a public blockchain. Several open source tools are available, obviating the need to use a third-party service. The second method is to create a smart contract that manages individual transactions and adds them into the public blockchain.

Decentralized Application Architecture

Decentralized applications, or dApps, are a novel way to deploy web-based applications with the program's logic encoded in smart contracts. In a typical application, you would deploy a web application in a cloud environment that holds storage, program logic, server instances, and front-end style sheets. With dApps, program (or smart contract) logic resides not in the cloud but in a public blockchain such as Ethereum and is encoded in smart contracts, as Figure 17.3 shows. In a way, dApps are the user interfaces for smart contracts. To transfer tokens or gas, the dApp may interact with well-known wallets such as MetaMask. Using the wallet, funds transfers are initiated, and transaction confirmations from the underlying blockchain are obtained.

dApps are novel because they are meant to be censorship resistant and built on a paradigm that contradicts how we have deployed traditional or centralized applications. Although there is no official definition of what a dApp is, they must meet the following criteria[7]:

- The application must be open source and operate autonomously with no single entity controlling most of its tokens, native or otherwise. Tokens represent incentives for users to interact with the application as well as for rewards to maintain it.
- Changes in the application's protocols must be decided by consensus of its users through various voting and staking mechanisms.
- The application's data and ledger must be stored in a public blockchain to avoid central points of failure. The application may create their own public blockchain infrastructure or use an existing one. Most dApps that exist today are built on existing blockchain infrastructure such as Ethereum and Tron, among others.

Traditional companies will find it difficult to convert their existing customer-facing applications into a dApp. The first value proposition for

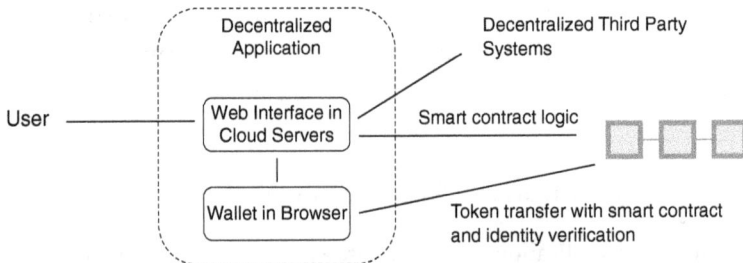

Figure 17.3 Logical structure of decentralization applications

---

[7]E. Vollstadt. "What are dApps," *Bitnation.* https://blog.bitnation.co/what-are-dapps/, (accessed March 10, 2020).

creating a dApp rests in the fact that the application is open source, allowing the company to gain traction faster using tokens as incentives and create a developer community around it. The second value proposition is its censorship-resistant nature. Unless the application has potential political sensitivity in its operation such as opinion sites, gambling, and prediction markets, being censorship resistant may not be important. The third value proposition is not having a central point of failure with regard to utilizing an underlying ledger. Shutting down a public blockchain network has reached a level of impossibility.

The fourth, and most important, value proposition, in my opinion, is the fact that building and deploying the application on existing public blockchain with economic incentives is comparatively less expensive than building a centralized application. This is because the back end, or ledger, is already built for you and does not need language-based customization.

With all these value propositions, the use of dApps must be growing exponentially, right? The result is a mixed bag. According to the dApp reporting website, State of the dApps, as of April 2020 there were only approximately 3,500 dApps (about 1,000 of them are deprecated) and 73,000 daily active users. The number of active dApp users in 2019 has doubled since 2018, from 1.5 to 3 million.[8] While the active user and total user numbers are not impressive, the number of transactions increased from 280 million to 3 billion from 2018 to 2019.

The largest growth of dApps from users has been in so-called "high-risk" applications such as decentralized finance, gambling, crypto exchange, and prediction. These also happen to be tightly regulated and strictly enforced industries in jurisdictions around the world. Perhaps that's the point. Let's build global, unstoppable, censorship-resistant applications that people can still participate in without running the risk of legal repercussions. This begs the question, is it worth building a general-purpose dApp with little or no legal risks if the probability of gaining traction is so low? For now, there seems to be a clear trade-off between being decentralized and exponential growth, fundraising. Remember Mr. Buterin's decentralization trilemma?

---

[8]Dapp. January 20, 2020. "2019 Annual Dapp Market Report," *Dapp.* https://www.dapp.com/article/dapp-com-2019-annual-dapp-market-report.

Hybrid Implementation Architecture

It is understandable and perfectly acceptable that enterprises will find it extremely difficult, and almost impossible, to suddenly convert their system from centralized to dApps. However, companies can leverage third-party decentralized services such as decentralized storage and smart contracts, making them an integral part of existing infrastructure. Figure 17.4 shows how traditional businesses can leverage innovative decentralized services on top of their existing infrastructure.

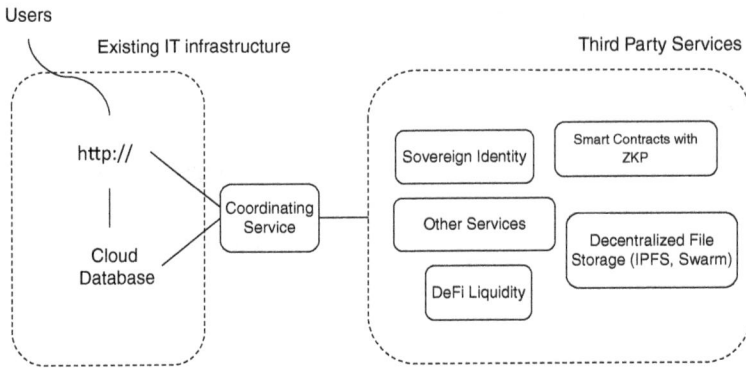

Figure 17.4 Existing infrastructure can connect with many external decentralized services

It is important to note that some of these third-party service providers are not fully decentralized and are heavily promoted by core developers employed or contracted by startups and foundations. Hence, these services may shut down for the same reasons that any other business does. Also, protocols that support these services are developing at a fast pace, making it important to keep up with version updates.

This hybrid architecture, which combines existing infrastructure with public blockchain infrastructure, will not be fully censorship resistant or without a central point of failure. This implementation is very close to using private blockchain. However, this architecture can be a pathway to decentralization and for companies to leverage public or consortium blockchain to realize the benefits of smart contracts, providing services such as transparency and accountability to customers.

If a new system is built for a consortium of multiple competing or collaborating entities, then the system can include a foundational layer with access to public blockchain to store transactions between the stakeholders. The blockchain will also enforce governance among the stakeholders. The architecture will include components such as cloud database and storage, identity, and access management.

Epilogue

This book lays the foundations of blockchain and the innovative business models that come with industrialization of trust or trust at scale. It provides the c-suite and senior executives with a playbook to help them embark on a journey to implement blockchain solutions in their operations and, on the way, future-proof their products and offerings. Blockchain is so nascent that there are few reference implementations, best practices, guidebooks, and best sellers to help us make those decisions.

I am constantly learning from dialogues with my peers, blog posts, and conferences where individuals debate about everything from protocols, smart contracts, currency predictions, and issues and challenges that lie ahead. This book is a collection of what I know and have experienced as a blockchain evangelist, consultant, and cofounder of a blockchain startup building a platform to solve one of the most difficult sectors—logistics and supply chain. It is difficult to build a platform on nascent blockchain technology for a traditional industry of moving freight because the platform must work for now and not a decade into the future. I am sure you'll experience the same.

It is abundantly clear that blockchain will disrupt fundamental components of trade and governance. The impact of such disruption is still being analyzed and debated. Blockchain is an exponential innovation that takes years and decades to unfold its true potential. After decades of centralization of services provided to us, the future of decentralization is here. However, it would be naïve to think everything will be decentralized or needs to be. Most businesses will be built on top of decentralized services and will exercise a certain measure of control over their institutions.

In the next few decades, as Fabrizio Romano Genovese wrote in "Poetry of Blockchain….", "… blockchain poetry will eventually die, take its natural course like many other technologies that came before us."[1] But

---

[1] F.R. Genovese. January 4, 2019. "The Poetry of Blockchain – A Celebration of Lateral Thinking," Medium Corporation. https://blog.statebox.org/the-poetry-of-blockchain-a-celebration-of-lateral-thinking-ee43c6e261a6.

we have a chance to delay the process, to spreserve it longer, and use it to benefit the future generations as much as we can.

Much work needs to be done to harness the power of blockchain for the benefit of future generations, and we are just getting started. Reducing the cost of trust is not trivial. That is one reason I think blockchain will follow an evolutionary path over decades. We are gradually preparing to thin the layer of trust that sits heavily between institutions and processes.

Until blockchain, we needed those thick layers of trust to facilitate commerce and economy. Those layers of trust reduced friction between parties. In return, entities who provided trust figured out that they could get away with overvaluing themselves. Intermediaries, regulators, standardized protocols, and so forth provided trust to businesses. Blockchain will not remove those "traditional" methods of trust. It will ignore them.

Glossary

Consensus mechanism is an integral part of the protocol that defines and ensures a majority of the nodes in the network are synchronized and agree on the state of the ledger. Without the consensus mechanism, blockchain cannot maintain immutability and be tamper evident. Proof of Work was the first widely known consensus mechanism proposed by Satoshi Nakamoto in the Bitcoin white paper in 2008. Since then, many versions of consensus mechanisms have been proposed and developed, including Proof of Stake, Proof of Authority, and so forth.

Crypto assets are digital assets that live on blockchain, meaning they are created, registered, and transacted using blockchain. Crypto assets include digital currencies or cryptocurrencies. They do not include physical assets that are tokenized on blockchain or virtual currencies such as PayPal, gaming points.

Cryptographic hash is a mathematical algorithm that takes any arbitrary digital data and produces a fixed-size enciphered text, called a hash or a hash value. Cryptographic hash functions are basic tools for modern cryptography. In blockchain, human readable transactions are converted to hashes and added to the blockchain.

Cryptogovernance, or tokenized governance, involves creating and modifying protocols of a blockchain network using smart contracts by the token holders of the protocol. Cryptogovernance is an emerging topic in the blockchain space owing to the emergence of decentralized autonomous organizations (DAOs), which, clearly, do not have the traditional structure of corporate entities and let the token holders govern the underlying protocol.

Decentralized identity, or DID, is a globally unique identifier that neither requires a centralized registration authority nor is created by such authority. DIDs are created by the individuals themselves in the form of public and private keys. The DID emphasizes the concept of self-sovereignty of the identity, and the individual has all the responsibilities of maintaining it.

Double spending is a problem in which someone tries to spend or pledge the same asset twice or to two different buyers at the same time. Banks prevent their customers from being able to double spend or send the same transaction twice to a recipient by taking custody and managing the customer's ledger. In blockchain, preventing double spending is nontrivial owing to the absence of centralized authority. It is also used to define a definitive attack by one or more participants of the network to double spend an asset by tampering with the underlying ledger.

Ethereum virtual machine is a sandboxed virtual stack embedded within each full Ethereum node in the network. It is responsible for executing smart contracts, which are typically written in higher-level languages, like Solidity.

Foundational technologies provide building blocks or foundations to build transformative applications and businesses. They often take a long time to adopt, scale, and mature. However, it has a lasting and multidomain impact. Examples of foundational technology include electricity, telecommunication, and the Internet.

Information asymmetry is defined as a difference between the amount/quality/ timing of information present between two contracting parties at a given time. For example, a buyer of an asset often has less information about the true condition of the asset. The buyer, on the other hand, may have more information about the true market value of the same asset.

Initial coin offering (ICO) is a method, which peaked in 2017–2018, for blockchain startups to raise funds by issuing coins, in many cases without requiring regulatory approvals. Coins typically do not represent commodities or assets, and are hence different from tokens.

Minting tokens refers to creating a smart contract with a predefined total supply of tokens to raise funds and incentivize users. Minting is done by contract code that also includes a logic of when and how many tokens are released to the public.

Off chain and on chain is a way of defining whether the transaction or information is stored in blockchain or traditional enterprise systems. When not stored in blockchain, the information is defined as stored off chain and vice versa. The terms off chain and on chain also denote whether certain actions were executed on blockchain or not. For example, on chain governance means voting by the token holders is executed by a governance smart contract.

Protocols include a set of rules, often defined in and enforced by smart contracts, for the network and the participants to adhere to. Both private and public blockchain creators define such rules to add transactions to the underlying ledger, to describe block creation, define incentives to miners, and for the nodes to agree on the consensus mechanism. Rules may be modified in the future by majority consensus of token holders or stakeholders.

Self-execution of smart contracts refers to the fact that the contract codes that reside in the public and permissionless blockchain don't require human or machine triggers to execute. The contract executes when it receives proper gas fees with a transaction submitted by a signed address.

Token generation events involve release of tokens to the general public and investors by the developers of a protocol and decentralized applications in order to raise funds. Token generation events are slightly different from ICOs in that the difference is between tokens and coins. Tokens mostly resting on blockchain are programmable and tradable representations of assets or utilities.

Transaction validator in the context of private blockchain means an entity known to the network's participants and trusted to validate transactions against the predefined protocol. In essence, the validator is staking its reputation and identity instead of resources as in Proof of Work or Proof of Stake. Unlike in the previously mentioned consensus mechanisms, the validator in a private network may or may not be incentivized by issuing tokens.

Trust machine means the technology or method that allows participants to use it as a trust layer to transact with other participants. Blockchain is often labeled as a trust machine because it provides a tamper-evident ledger of transactions between the participants.

Two-way peg is a method to transfer one cryptocurrency to another and vice versa. Typically, this occurs between Bitcoin and an alternative cryptocurrency using a sidechain. When two currencies exchange, no currency is "transferred" between the two blockchain. When a user converts Bitcoin to another coin, the same value of Bitcoin is locked in the Bitcoin blockchain, and the same amount of alternative cryptocurrency is unlocked in the sidechain.

Wallet or crypto wallet can be a hardware device or an application that stores public and private keys. Recently, wallets have evolved to provide additional functions such as logging into blockchain and signing transactions to interact with smart contracts.

About the Author

Rajat Rajbhandari, PhD is a cofounder of dexFreight, which is pioneering the use of blockchain in logistics. Also, as a working group lead, he manages the supply chain and vehicle identity working groups at the Mobility Open Blockchain Initative. He works with large auto manufacturers, suppliers, and technology vendors to build standards, and reference implementation for the industry. His work on blockchain has been covered by *Wall Street Journal, International Business Times, Freightwaves, Journal of Commerce*, and many others. Rajat began his career as a research scientist at the Texas A&M Transportation Institute.

Index

BUSINESS LAW AND CORPORATE RISK MANAGEMENT COLLECTION

John Wood, *Editor*

- *Guerrilla Warfare in the Corporate Jungle: Adaptations for Survival* by K.F. Dochartaigh
- *Successful Cybersecurity Professionals: How To Change Your Behavior to Protect Your Organization* by Steven Brown
- *Artificial Intelligence for Security* by Archie Addo
- *Artificial Intelligence Design and Solution for Risk and Security* by Archie Addo
- *Artificial Intelligence for Risk Management* by Archie Addo
- *The Business-Minded CISCO: How to Organize, Evangelize, and Operate an Enterprise-wide IT Risk Management Program* by Bryan C. Kissinger
- *Getting the Best Equipment Lease Deal: An Equipment Leasing Guide for Lessees* by Richard M.Contino
- *Equipment Leasing and Financing: A Product Sales and Business Profit Center Strategy* by Richard M. Contino
- *AI Concepts for Business Applications* by Nelson E. Brestoff
- *How New Risk Management Helps Leaders Master Uncertainty* by Robert B. Pojasek
- *Understanding Cyberrisks in IoT: When Smart Things Turn Against You* by Carolina A. Adaros Boye
- *The Business of Cybersecurity: Foundations and Ideologies* by Ashwini Sathnur
- *Cybersecurity Law: Protect Yourself and Your Customers* by Shimon Brathwaite
- *Conversations in Cyberspace* by Giulio D'Agostino
- *Board-Seeker: Your Guidebook and Career Map into the Corporate Boardroom* by Ralph Ward
- *Contract Law: A Comparison of Civil Law and Common Law Jurisdictions* by Claire-Michelle Smyth

Concise and Applied Business Books

The Collection listed above is one of 30 business subject collections that Business Expert Press has grown to make BEP a premiere publisher of print and digital books. Our concise and applied books are for...

- Professionals and Practitioners
- Faculty who adopt our books for courses
- Librarians who know that BEP's Digital Libraries are a unique way to offer students ebooks to download, not restricted with any digital rights management
- Executive Training Course Leaders
- Business Seminar Organizers

Business Expert Press books are for anyone who needs to dig deeper on business ideas, goals, and solutions to everyday problems. Whether one print book, one ebook, or buying a digital library of 110 ebooks, we remain the affordable and smart way to be business smart. For more information, please visit **www.businessexpertpress.com**, or contact **sales@businessexpertpress.com**.